PASTA COOKBOOK

Prepare Your Favorite Pasta Dishes With Delicious Pasta Recipes

(A Pasta Cookbook Everyone Loves!)

Tracy Elder

Published by Alex Howard

© **Tracy Elder**

All Rights Reserved

Pasta Cookbook: Prepare Your Favorite Pasta Dishes With Delicious Pasta Recipes (A Pasta Cookbook Everyone Loves!)

ISBN 978-1-990169-05-2

All rights reserved. No part of this guide may be reproduced in any form without permission in writing from the publisher except in the case of brief quotations embodied in critical articles or reviews.

Legal & Disclaimer

The information contained in this book is not designed to replace or take the place of any form of medicine or professional medical advice. The information in this book has been provided for educational and entertainment purposes only.

The information contained in this book has been compiled from sources deemed reliable, and it is accurate to the best of the Author's knowledge; however, the Author cannot guarantee its accuracy and validity and cannot be held liable for any errors or omissions. Changes are periodically made to this book. You must consult your doctor or get professional medical advice before using any of the suggested remedies, techniques, or information in this book.

Table of contents

PART 1 1

CHAPTER 1: SEAFOOD PASTA 2

RECIPE 1: SPAGHETTI WITH CLAMS 2

RECIPE 2: ORANGE-BALSAMIC SHRIMP PASTA 5

RECIPE 3: SPAGHETTI WITH TROUT CARBONARA 8

RECIPE 4: SHRIMP FRA DIAVOLO 10

RECIPE 5: SPAGHETTI WITH LOBSTER 14

RECIPE 6: SPAGHETTI AL TONNO 17

RECIPE 7: SPAGHETTI WITH CHICORY, ANCHOVIES, AND BREADCRUMBS 19

RECIPE 8: SPAGHETTI ALLA PUTTANESCA 23

RECIPE 9: SPAGHETTI WITH BACCALÀ (SALT COD) ALLA GHIOTTA 25

RECIPE 10: SPAGHETTI AND SQUID IN SQUID INK SAUCE 28

CHAPTER 2: MEAT PASTA 31

RECIPE 11: YIAYIA'S TRADITIONAL SPAGHETTI BOLOGNESE 31

RECIPE 12: BACON, CHILI AND FETA SPAGHETTI 34

RECIPE 13: TACO SPAGHETTI 36

RECIPE 14: BAKED SPAGHETTI CASSEROLE 39

RECIPE 15: SPAGHETTI WITH CRUSHED PEAS, MINT AND PANCETTA 42

Recipe 16: Cajun Chicken Spaghetti 45

Recipe 17: Nonna's Traditional Spaghetti Bolognese 48

Recipe 18: Corsican Spaghetti 51

Recipe 19: Fresh Pasta With Lamb And Bell Pepper Sauce 53

Recipe 20: Eggplant And Country Ham Ragù 57

CHAPTER 3: VEGETARIAN PASTA 61

Recipe 21: Spring Vegetable Alfredo 61

Recipe 22: Cacio E Pepe 64

Recipe 23: Spanish Spaghetti 67

Recipe 24: Caprese Spaghetti 69

Recipe 25: Spaghetti In A Blush Sauce 71

Recipe 26: Chocolate Spaghetti 73

Recipe 27: Spaghetti With Four Cheeses 75

Recipe 28: French Spaghetti 77

Recipe 29: Spaghetti With Artichokes, Pine Nuts, And Pesto 80

Recipe 30: Morel And Asparagus Spaghetti 82

Recipe 31: Spaghetti Salad 85

Recipe 32: Red Pesto Spaghetti 87

Recipe 33: Spaghetti Primavera 89

Recipe 34: Red-Wine Spaghetti With Walnuts And Parsley 92

Recipe 35: Spaghetti Napoli 95

RECIPE 36: RICOTTA SPAGHETTI	97
RECIPE 37: SPAGHETTI GENOVESE	99
RECIPE 38: ROCKET SPAGHETTI	102
RECIPE 39: SPAGHETTI AGLIO E OLIO	104
RECIPE 40: SPAGHETTI ALLA VESUVIANA	107
PART 2	**110**
MAKING YOUR OWN HOMEMADE PASTA	111
EGG NOODLES	113
BASIC PASTA	115
GRANDMA'S NOODLES I	116
GRANDMA'S NOODLES II	117
FRESH SEMOLINA AND EGG PASTA	119
GRANDMA'S BUTTER NOODLES	121
HOMEMADE FOUR CHEESE RAVIOLI	123
HOMEMADE NOODLES	127
WHOLE WHEAT PASTA	128
HOMEMADE EGG NOODLES	130
CHICKEN AND SPINACH RAVIOLI	131
PUMPKIN RAVIOLI	134
A FAREWELL TO BASIL FETTUCCINE	137
FRESH PASTA	139

Eggless Pasta 141

Granny's Homemade Noodles 143

Badische Schupfnudeln (Potato Noodles) 145

Unique Spinach Noodles 147

Spinach, Feta, And Pine Nut Ravioli Filling 149

Smoked Salmon Ravioli 151

Spaetzle II 154

Genuine Egg Noodles 155

Plain Pasta 157

Pasta For Don And His Loves 159

Spelt Noodles 161

Vareniky 163

Papa Oriold's Spaetzle 166

Chestnut Pasta 168

Grandma Randolph's Noodles 171

Herb Spaetzle 173

MOM'S PASTA DOUGH 175

Old School Pasta Dough 177

Easy Homemade Pasta Dough 179

Tomato Sauce With Sausage 181

Tomatocream Vodka Sauce For Pasta 182

Tommys Tomato Gravy 183

Turkey Bolognese Recipe 184

Turkey Pasta Sauce 186

Tuscan Sausage Ragu 187

Versatile Tomato Sauce 189

Part 1

Chapter 1: Seafood Pasta

Recipe 1: Spaghetti With Clams

Spaghetti alle vongole, to give it its Italian name, is a popular dish from Campania in southern Italy. It is without a doubt one of the best spaghetti seafood dishes, ever!

Yield: 4

Preparation Time: **25mins**

Cook Time: **25mins**

Total Cooking Time: **50mins**

Ingredient List:
- 2 pounds fresh clams

- 1 tablespoon cornmeal
- Salt
- 1 pound uncooked spaghetti
- 8 tablespoons virgin olive oil
- 3 cloves garlic (peeled, cut into slivers)
- 3 small dried Italian pepperoncini
- Black pepper
- 1 large handful fresh flat-leaf parsley (chopped)

Instructions:

1. First, thoroughly clean the clams, throwing away any that have broken shells, or don't close when you tap them. Place them in a large mixing bowl filled with cold water, along with the cornmeal for 30 minutes. Drain, rinse and wash away any sand or debris.

2. In a large pan of boiling salted water, cook the spaghetti according to the package instructions.

3. In the meantime, in a large and heavy frying pan, over low heat, heat the oil. Add the garlic slivers along with the pepperoncini and cook until the garlic emits its fragrance, without browning.

4. Increase the heat to moderate, and add the clams, shaking and swirling the pan in order to evenly coat the clams in the oil and garlic.

5. Add a generous amount of seasoning and scatter in the parsley, tossing to coat the clams.

6. Cover the pan with a secure lid and cook, while shaking the occasionally shaking the pan, for 3 minutes, or until the clams are cooked and open. Discard any unopened clams.

7. As soon as the spaghetti and clams are sufficiently cooked, drain the spaghetti and add it to the clams, once again tossing to combine.

8. Garnish with chopped parsley and serve.

Recipe 2: Orange-Balsamic Shrimp Pasta

Sautéed shrimp in a tangy orange citrus sauce is amazing.

Yield: 4

Preparation Time: **15mins**

Cook Time: **10mins**

Total Cooking Time: **25mins**

Ingredient List:
- Salt
- 12 ounces uncooked fine spaghetti
- 1 pound raw shrimp (thawed, peeled, deveined)
- 1 tablespoon cornstarch
- ¼ teaspoons red pepper flakes (crushed)
- ⅛ teaspoons cayenne pepper
- ½ teaspoons freshly ground black pepper
- ⅓ cup balsamic vinegar (preferable golden)
- 2 cups freshly squeezed orange juice

- 6 garlic cloves (minced)
- 1 tablespoon olive oil
- 2 tablespoons unsalted butter
- ¼ cup fresh parsley (chopped)

Instructions:

1. Bring a deep pan of salted water to boil and cook the pasta according to the package instructions. Using a colander drain, and set to one side.

2. Meanwhile, using kitchen paper towel, pat the shrimp dry, leaving tails on.

3. In a large mixing bowl, add the cornstarch, along with the pepper flakes, cayenne pepper, and black pepper. Add the vinegar, whisking to combine, until the cornstarch is totally dissolved.

4. Whisk in the freshly squeezed orange juice and minced garlic and set to one side.

5. In a large, stainless steel saucepan over moderate to high heat, warm the oil together with 1 tablespoon of butter.

6. Add the shrimp in a single layer, and sear for 60 seconds.

7. Using kitchen tongs, flip the shrimp over and cook for another couple minutes or until the shrimp are opaque.

8. Using a slotted kitchen utensil, transfer the cooked shrimp to a warmed plate.

9. Add the orange juice mixture to the saucepan and increase the temperature to high, bring to a gentle simmer and cook for approximately 60 seconds, to slightly thicken.

10. Add, while stirring the remaining butter, the cooked spaghetti, shrimp, and parsley. Tossing well to evenly coat.

11. Serve in bowls and enjoy garnished with chopped parsley.

Recipe 3: Spaghetti With Trout Carbonara

When we think of Carbonara, it's usually ham that springs to mind, but for fish lovers this trout version is ideal.

Yield: 4

Preparation Time: **5mins**

Cook Time: **25mins**

Total Cooking Time: **30mins**

Ingredient List:
- Salt
- 11 ounces uncooked spaghetti
- 2 medium eggs (beaten)
- 5½ ounces fresh cream
- 5½ ounces fresh trout
- Zest of 1 lemon (divided)
- ¼ cup butter

- Ground black pepper

Instructions:

1. In a deep pan, of boiling salted water, cook the spaghetti until al dente. Drain.

2. In a large pan, slowly reduce the fresh cream over low heat until it reduces by around half, add the beaten eggs and cook, while continually stirring, until the sauce begins to thicken. Using a hand blender, emulsify.

3. Prepare the trout by removing its skin, and cut it into bite-sized pieces, and fry the fish in butter until it begins to change color.

4. Add the cooked pasta to the pan and mix, along with ⅔ of the grated lemon zest.

5. Pour a small amount of the egg-cream mixture onto the bottom of each bowl and pile the spaghetti and trout on top.

6. Grate additional lemon zest on the top along with a sprinkling of black pepper.

7. Serve.

Recipe 4: Shrimp Fra Diavolo

You can take away a little of the spice in this recipe by adding or subtracting the amount of red chili flakes you use.

Yield: 4

Preparation Time: **25mins**

Cook Time: **30mins**

Total Cooking Time: **55mins**

Ingredient List:
- Sea salt
- ¾ pound medium shrimp (shelled, deveined, shells reserved)
- Large pinch baking soda
- 6 tablespoons extra-virgin olive oil (divided)
- 4 medium garlic cloves (thinly sliced)
- 1½ teaspoons dried oregano

- 1-2 teaspoons red chili flakes
- 2 tablespoons brandy
- 1 (28-ounce) can whole peeled tomatoes and their juices (coarsely pureed)
- ½ cup bottled clam juice
- 1 pound uncooked spaghetti
- ¼ cup minced flat-leaf parsley leaves plus tender stems

Instructions:

1. Bring a pot of boiling salted water to a rapid boil.

2. In a mixing bowl, toss the shrimp together with ½ a teaspoon of sea salt, and a large pinch of baking powder. Set to one side.

3. In a large frying pan, over moderate to high heat, heat 4 tablespoons of olive oil until it begins to shimmer.

4. Add the shrimp shells reserved during preparation, and cook, while continually stirring, until they are a reddish color, approximately 3-4 minutes.

5. Remove the pan from the heat, and using kitchen tongs, remove the shells, allowing excess oil to drip back into the pan; throw the shells away.

6. Return the pan to a moderate to high heat, and add the shrimp, cook, while occasionally turning and stirring, until the shrimp have brown spots and are nearly fully cooked, this will take a few minutes.

7. Remove the pan from the heat and transfer the shrimp to a serving plate, and set to one side.

8. Return the pan to a moderate to low heat and add the garlic, along with the oregano, and chili flakes, and cook, while stirring, until the garlic begins to turn a light golden color, 2-3 minutes.

9. Add the brandy, and cook until it is has almost totally evaporated. Add the tomatoes and pour in the clam juice bring to a simmer and season well with sea salt.

10. In a large pan of boiling salted water cook, the spaghetti, until it is al dente, 6-8 minutes.

11. Drain the pasta, and reserve 1 cup of cooking water.

12. Add the cooked spaghetti to the sauce together with a splash of the cooking water.

13. Add the shrimp and continue cooking over moderate to high heat, stirring continually, until the sauce reduces and sticks to the pasta, and the shrimp are sufficiently heated through. Add a drop more cooking water if necessary.

14. Add the parsley along with the remaining olive oil and serve.

Recipe 5: Spaghetti With Lobster

If you are fortunate enough to have ever visited Venice then you are sure to have tried Spaghetti all'Astice. Fresh lobster, tossed with garlic, juicy red tomatoes and dry white wine – buon appetito.

Yield: 4

Preparation Time: **10mins**

Cook Time: **30mins**

Total Cooking Time: **40mins**

Ingredient List:
- 1 pound live Maine lobster
- 3 tablespoons virgin olive oil
- 1 garlic clove (peeled, minced)
- 1 cup Italian dry white wine
- 4 large, ripe tomatoes (cored, chopped)
- Salt and black pepper

- 12 ounces spaghetti
- 4 sprigs parsley (trimmed, chopped)

Instructions:

1. Kill the lobster as quickly as possible, by plunging a sharp kitchen knife into the top of its head, just behind the eyes, chop into between 8 and 10 pieces.

2. In a frying pan or skillet over moderate to high heat, heat the olive oil.

3. Add the pieces of lobster along with any juices and the garlic, and cook while stirring. Turn the lobsters over during cooking and cook for 60 seconds.

4. Add the dry white wine and cook until the wine has evaporated, for around 2-3 minutes.

5. Add the chopped tomatoes and cook, occasionally stirring. Using the back of a wooden spoon, break the tomatoes down, and cook until the sauce thickens and becomes smooth; 8-10 minutes. Season well with salt and black pepper.

6. In the meantime, cook the spaghetti, over high heat in a large pan of boiling salted water until it has a bite (al dente), 8-10 minutes.

7. Using a colander, drain the spaghetti, return it to the pan, and add the sauce, stirring to combine. Continue cooking for 2-3 minutes to heat through and serve garnished with chopped parsley.

Recipe 6: Spaghetti Al Tonno

From pot to plate in half an hour a delicious midweek meal for the whole family.

Yield: 4

Preparation Time: **10mins**

Cook Time: **20mins**

Total Cooking Time: **30mins**

Ingredient List:
- Sea salt
- 8 ounces uncooked spaghetti (cooked, drained)
- 4 tablespoons olive oil
- 1 large garlic clove (minced)
- 1 shallot (minced)
- 2 anchovies
- 1 (14½ ounce) canned, crushed tomatoes
- Crushed red pepper flakes
- 1 (7 ounce) can tuna in olive oil (drained, flaked)

- ¼ cup Italian parsley (chopped)
- Black pepper

Instructions:

1. Bring a deep pot of boiling, lightly salted water to the boil and, cook the spaghetti, according to the package instructions, until it is al dente. Drain.

2. In a skillet or frying pan, over moderate heat, heat the olive oil.

3. Add the minced garlic along with the shallot, and anchovies to the frying pan and cook while stirring for 60 seconds.

4. Add the crushed tomatoes, together with the red pepper flakes, and simmer for 15 minutes, reducing the heat if necessary.

5. Add the tuna and stir to combine. Remove the pan from the heat.

6. Add the drained spaghetti and parsley and toss to incorporate.

7. Sprinkle with black pepper and serve.

Recipe 7: Spaghetti With Chicory, Anchovies, And Breadcrumbs

Spaghetti con puntarelle, acciughe e briciole, is a dish of spaghetti with a sauce made of puntarelle (a variant of chicory), anchovy, breadcrumbs, and garlic.

Yield: 4

Preparation Time: **5mins**

Cook Time: **20mins**

Total Cooking Time: **25mins**

Ingredient List:
- 8 medium garlic cloves (divided)
- 5 ounces sourdough (crust removed, cut into 1" pieces)
- 1 teaspoon lemon zest (finely grated)
- Sea salt
- Black pepper

- ¼ cup + 3 tablespoons olive oil
- ½ teaspoons crushed red pepper flakes
- 4 anchovy fillets packed in oil
- 1 tablespoon + freshly squeezed lemon juice
- 14 ounces uncooked spaghetti
- 2 ounces Pecorino (finely grated)
- ½ cup parsley (finely chopped)
- 2 tablespoons unsalted butter

Instructions:

1. Slice half of the cloves of garlic very finely, and put to one side.

2. Ina food processor pulse the remaining cloves until chopped finely. Add the pieces of sourdough bread along with the lemon zest and process on pulse until a coarse crumb consistency is achieved. Season well and set aside.

3. In a heavy pan or Dutch oven, over moderate heat, heat ¼ cup of olive oil and cook the set-aside breadcrumb mixture, while continually stirring, until crisp and golden, approximately 4-5 minutes. Using a slotted kitchen utensil, transfer the breadcrumb mixture to a mixing bowl.

4. Using the same pan, over moderate to low heat, heat the remaining olive oil. Cook the reserved garlic, occasionally stirring, until the edges are golden, for around 60 seconds.

5. Add the pepper flakes and anchovies and cook, while stirring, until the anchovies totally dissolve, around 60 seconds. Add the lemon juice and stir to combine.

6. In the meantime, cook the spaghetti in a large pan of salted, boiling water, occasionally stirring, until it is al dente, for a few minutes less than the manufacturer's instructions. Drain and set aside 1 cup of cooking water.

7. Using kitchen tongs, transfer the spaghetti to the pan with the sauce along with 1 cup of cooking water.

8. Cook, while tossing frequently. Add an additional 3 tablespoons of cooking water and gradually add the Pecorino, gently tossing until it is emulsified and melted.

9. Remove the pan from the heat, and add the parsley, along with the unsalted butter and 50% of the

breadcrumb mixture and toss until the butter is totally melted and incorporated.

10. If the pasta is still a little dry, pour in a drop more cooking water and olive oil and once again, toss.

11. Season with salt and pepper, and additional lemon juice.

12. Divide the pasta between individual bowls and scatter any remaining breadcrumb mixture over the top.

Recipe 8: Spaghetti Alla Puttanesca

This spicy pasta dish originated in the mid 20th century in Naples and is the perfect go-to family meal.

Yield: 4

Preparation Time: **10mins**

Cook Time: **15mins**

Total Cooking Time: **25mins**

Ingredient List:
- Salt
- 14 ounces uncooked spaghetti
- Olive oil
- 4 cloves garlic (peeled, thinly sliced)
- 3 anchovy fillets (chopped)
- 2 fresh red chili's (seeds not removed, sliced)
- Handful of black olives (pitted)
- 2 handfuls ripe cherry tomatoes (halved)
- Small bunch of fresh basil (leaves picked)

- Parmesan (grated, to serve)

Instructions:

1. In a pan of boiling salted water, cook the spaghetti according to the manufacturer's directions. Drain the spaghetti, setting aside 1 cupful of cooking water.

2. In the meantime, place a frying pan or skillet over a moderate to high heat.

3. Add a good glug of oil, together with the garlic, anchovy and chilies.

4. Tear in the pitted olives and stir for a couple of minutes or until the garlic is golden and the anchovy melt into the base.

5. Add the tomatoes, along with a good splash of cooking water, and cover with a tight-fitting lid. Cook for 3-4 minutes, or until the tomatoes begin to cook down and add the basil to the sauce along followed by the cooking water. Taste and season.

6. Transfer to a serving dish and sprinkle with Parmesan.

Recipe 9: Spaghetti With Baccalà (Salt Cod) Alla Ghiotta

Salted cod is particularly popular in Italy. It is relatively inexpensive and very versatile. Ask your fishmonger to prepare it for you.

Yield: 4

Preparation Time: **15mins**

Cook Time: **35mins**

Total Cooking Time: **50mins**

Ingredient List:
- 2 tablespoons capers
- 3 tablespoons olive oil
- 1 medium onion (peeled, finely chopped)
- 2 medium celery stalks (finely chopped)
- 1¾ ounces green olive (pitted)
- 10 cherry tomatoes (halved)

- 10½ ounces passata
- 1 pound 5 ounces salt cod (prepared)
- Pepper
- 4 medium potatoes (peeled, chopped)
- 14 ounces uncooked spaghetti

Instructions:

1. First, put the capers in a mixing bowl.

2. In a skillet or frying pan, heat the oil. Add the chopped onion, celery, pitted olives, and capers and cook until the onion is translucent.

3. Add the tomatoes, and when they are beginning to soften, add the passata.

4. Cut the prepared cod into medium size pieces and add to the sauce.

5. Cook everything on a moderate to high heat and cook for a few minutes. Season with pepper.

6. Add the chopped potatoes to the sauce, cover with a tight-fitting lid, and lower the heat. Continue cooking for 20-30 minutes or until the potatoes are fork tender

7. Meanwhile, cook the spaghetti until al dente in unsalted, boiling water according to the

manufacturer's directions. There is no need to add salt as the capers are already salty.

8. Transfer approximately half of the salted cod and the potatoes to a serving dish and cover with a lid to serve on the side.

9. Drain the spaghetti and add it to the remaining sauce, stir well to combine.

10. Serve!

Recipe 10: Spaghetti And Squid In Squid Ink Sauce

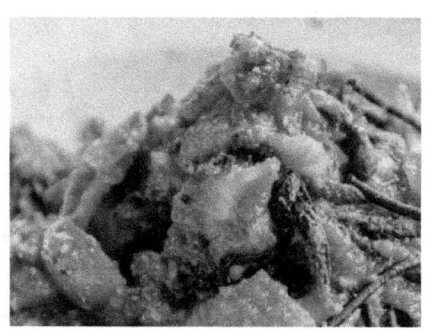

Spaghetti al Nero di Seppia has a tangy sea flavor, and the black sauce is made with either squid or cuttlefish ink. Your local fishmonger should be able to source the squid for you. This dramatic dish is guaranteed to impress your dinner guests.

Yield: 4

Preparation Time: **30mins**

Cook Time: 1hour 30mins

Total Cooking Time: **2hours**

Ingredient List:
- 1¼ pounds very fresh squid (un-cleaned)
- ¼ cup olive oil
- 2 garlic cloves (peeled, minced)

- 1 small bunch parsley (minced)
- Freshly ground black pepper
- 1 tablespoon tomato paste (diluted in a drop of water)
- ⅓ cup Italian dry white wine
- 1-2 tablespoons coarse sea salt
- ¾ pound uncooked spaghetti
- Fine sea salt (to taste)

HHHHHHHHHHHHHHHHHHHHHHHHHHHHHHHHHHHH HH

Instructions:

1. First, carefully clean the squid: You do this by separating the heads from the tentacles. Remove the squid's guts, and put the ink sacs to one side, it is important though, not to break or damage them.

2. Under cold running water, wash the squid, dice their bodies and chop their tentacles.

3. Over a small jug or bowl, open the sacs and collect the squid ink.

4. In a pan, over moderate heat, heat the oil and fry the garlic without browning.

5. Add the prepared squid, along with the parsley, and season generously with black pepper.

6. Cover the pan, with a lid, and over low heat, simmer for 45 minutes, checking every 7-10 minutes or so, to make sure that it isn't sticking. Add a drop of hot water if necessary.

7. As soon as the sauce has simmered, add the tomato paste, and white wine. Mix to combine and simmer, with no lid, for 20 minutes.

8. Add a drop of hot water to dilute the sauce, cover with a lid, and simmer for half an hour.

9. Half an hour before you are ready to serve, bring 3 quarts of water to boil, and add between 1 and 2 tablespoons of sea salt, stir. As soon as it returns to a rolling boil, add the spaghetti.

10. Immediately, but gradually, add the squid ink into the sauce and stir. Add the amount of ink depending on your preference.

11. After 8-10 minutes, the spaghetti is ready when it is al dente.

12. Using a colander, drain the spaghetti, and toss it in the sauce until it is evenly coated.

Chapter 2: Meat Pasta

Recipe 11: Yiayia's Traditional Spaghetti Bolognese

The answer to an Italian Bolognese; Macaronia me Kima, is a classic Greek dish of spaghetti and meat sauce. The Greek version brings a whole set of different flavors to the table with the addition of cinnamon, allspice, and cloves.

Yield: 4-6
Preparation Time: **10mins**
Cook Time: **45mins**
Total Cooking Time: **55mins**

Ingredient List:

- 3 tablespoons Greek olive oil
- 1 pound ground beef
- 1 medium onion (peeled, diced)
- 2 garlic cloves (peeled, finely minced)
- ¼ cup red wine
- 1 teaspoon ground cinnamon
- 3 berries allspices berries
- Pinch of ground cloves
- Salt and freshly ground black pepper
- ½ teaspoons sugar
- 1 (15 ounce) can tomato sauce
- 1 cup water
- ¼ cup fresh parsley (chopped)
- ½ tablespoons butter
- 1 pound uncooked spaghetti
- Mizithra, Kefalotyri* or Parmesan cheese (grated)

Instructions:

1. In a large saucepan (preferably 4-5 quart) over moderate to high heat, heat the oil. Add the beef and cook until browned with no pink remaining.

2. Add the onions and garlic and sauté until the onion becomes translucent and the garlic emits its fragrance, this will only take 60-90 seconds.

3. Pour in the red wine and allow to simmer for a couple minutes.

4. Next, add the cinnamon, along with the allspice, cloves, salt, black pepper, sugar, tomato sauce, and water.

5. Reduce the heat to low and while uncovered, simmer for 45 minutes, occasionally stirring. The sauce should be a meaty consistency with only a little juice.

6. Add the parsley together with ½ a tablespoon of butter**.

7. In a large pan of boiling salted water, prepare the spaghetti according to the package instructions, and until al dente.

8. Drain and serve topped with meat sauce, and sprinkled with grated cheese.

*Greek hard cheeses that can be found in many specialty delicatessens.

** It is not necessary but allowing the sauce to rest overnight, will help to develop and intensify the flavors.

Recipe 12: Bacon, Chili And Feta Spaghetti

Ready to serve in half an hour, this spicy spaghetti dish makes a perfect mid-week meal. Salty feta makes a welcome change to the more traditional Parmesan.

Yield: 2

Preparation Time: **15mins**

Cook Time: **15mins**

Total Cooking Time: **30mins**

Ingredient List:
- Salt
- 3½ ounces uncooked spaghetti
- 1½ tablespoons butter
- 2 slices bacon (cut into strips)
- ½ red chili pepper (deseeded, finely sliced)
- 2 teaspoons lime zest

- 1 tablespoon fresh basil leaves (finely chopped)
- Black pepper
- ½ cup feta cheese (crumbled)

Instructions:

1. Bring a large saucepan of salted water to the boil and cook the spaghetti according to the manufacturer's instructions, until it has a bite (al dente). Using a colander, drain, reserving ¼ cup of pasta cooking water, and put to one side.

2. In the meantime, in a wide frying pan or skillet melt the butter. Add the strips of bacon, and fry until sufficiently cooked.

3. Next, add the red chili pepper, and remove the pan from the heat.

4. Toss the cooked spaghetti along with the bacon and pasta cooking water.

5. Carefully, mix in the lime zest along with the basil.

6. Season well with salt and pepper and divide between 2 pasta bowls.

7. Crumble the feta cheese on top and serve.

Recipe 13: Taco Spaghetti

If the jury's out and you can't decide whether to go Italian or Mexican, then this spaghetti dish is the perfect choice!

Yield: 2

Preparation Time: **10mins**

Cook Time: **30mins**

Total Cooking Time: **40mins**

Ingredient List:
- Salt
- 8 ounces uncooked spaghetti
- 1 tablespoon virgin olive oil
- 1 pound premium ground beef
- 1 tablespoon taco seasoning
- 1 garlic clove (chopped)

- 1 can diced tomatoes and green chilies
- 1 tablespoon tomato paste
- ¼ cup canned, small diced tomatoes
- 3 cups water
- ½ cup Cheddar cheese (shredded)
- ½ cup mozzarella cheese (shredded)
- Fresh cilantro (chopped)

Instructions:

1. In a large pan of boiling salted water, cook the spaghetti according to the package instructions. Drain and set to one side.

2. In a frying pan or skillet, heat the oil over moderate to high heat.

3. Add the ground beef and cook until browned. Add the taco seasoning, stirring to combine and tilt the pan over the kitchen sink and drain away excess grease.

4. Add the garlic, diced tomatoes, and green chilies, along with the tomato paste, small diced tomatoes and water and simmer for 10-15 minutes.

5. Divide the spaghetti between individual bows, top with the sauce and scatter with the Cheddar and mozzarella cheese.

6. Allow the cheeses to melt before serving, garnished with chopped cilantro.

Recipe 14: Baked Spaghetti Casserole

This cheesy spaghetti casserole is sure to be a big hit.

Yield: 3-4

Preparation Time: **10mins**

Cook Time: **1hour**

Total Cooking Time: **1hour 10mins**

Ingredient List:

- Salt
- 10 ounces uncooked spaghetti
- 1 pound ground beef
- 1 (24 ounce) jar spaghetti sauce
- 1 cup sour cream
- 15 ounces ricotta cheese
- Freshly ground black pepper
- Parmesan cheese (freshly grated)
- Parsley (chopped, to garnish)

Instructions:

1. Preheat the main oven to 350 degrees F.

2. Bring a large saucepan of salted water to boil and cook the spaghetti according to the manufacturer's instructions. Drain and set to one side.

3. In a skillet or deep saucepan cook the beef until no pink remains, and then add one jar of your favorite spaghetti sauce and stir to combine. Set to one side.

4. In a large mixing bowl, toss the cooked spaghetti together with the sour cream and ricotta cheese. Season well with salt and freshly ground black pepper.

5. In a casserole dish, evenly spread approximately one third of the meat sauce on the base of the casserole dish. Lay the drained spaghetti on top. Top with the remaining (2/3) of meat sauce.

6. Scatter grated Parmesan over the top.

7. Cover the dish with aluminum foil and bake for 40-45 minutes, after which, remove the aluminum foil and return the oven for several minutes, or until the casserole is heated through and the cheese is melted.

8. Serve, garnished with a sprinkle of chopped parsley.

Recipe 15: Spaghetti With Crushed Peas, Mint And Pancetta

The perfect ménage a trois; peas, mint, and pancetta married together in a fresh and tasty spaghetti dish.

Yield: 4-6

Preparation Time: **15mins**

Cook Time: **22mins**

Total Cooking Time: **37mins**

Ingredient List:
- Salt
- 14 ounces uncooked spaghetti
- 3 tablespoons olive oil
- 3 ounces pancetta (diced)
- ¼ medium onion (peeled, finely chopped)
- 2 cloves garlic (peeled, finely chopped)
- 3 tablespoons Italian dry white wine
- ¾ cup chicken stock

- 9 ounces frozen peas
- ½ cup mint (torn)
- Pecorino pepato cheese (finely grated, to serve)

Instructions:

1. In a deep pan of boiling salted water, cook the spaghetti, until it is al dente, for 6-8 minutes. Using a colander drain, and return the pasta to the pot along with 2 tablespoons of the pasta cooking water.

2. In the meantime, over moderate to high heat, heat the olive oil in a large frying pan or skillet. Add the pancetta and cook for 3-4 minutes, or until it begins to crisp.

3. Add the onion along with the chopped garlic and fry for 3-4 minutes, until the onions begin to soften and the garlic emits its fragrance.

4. Deglaze the pan with the white wine, pour in the stock and bring to a gentle simmer.

5. Add the frozen peas, simmering until just tender, for between 2-4 minutes.

6. Remove the pan from the heat, season as needed and crush the peas.

7. Toss the frozen peas and torn mint through the cooked spaghetti, season to taste and scatter grated cheese on top.

Recipe 16: Cajun Chicken Spaghetti

An alternative take on the conventional shrimp pasta, but equally as good; super creamy rich sauce over tender chicken, with a Cajun kick.

Yield: 2-4

Preparation Time: **10mins**

Cook Time: **30mins**

Total Cooking Time: **40mins**

Ingredient List:
- Salt
- 7 ounces uncooked spaghetti
- 2 chicken breasts (cut into bite-sized cubes)
- 2½ teaspoons Cajun seasoning (divided)
- ¼ teaspoons paprika
- ¼ teaspoons freshly ground black pepper
- 1 tablespoon olive oil

- 1¼ cups chicken broth (divided)
- 1 tablespoon butter
- 1 tablespoon flour
- 1 cup mozzarella cheese (shredded)
- ½ cup heavy cream
- Tabasco (to taste)

Instructions:

1. Bring a large deep saucepan of salted water to boil, cook the spaghetti according to the package instructions. Drain and set aside.

2. In a large mixing bowl, add the cubes of chicken along with 2 teaspoons of Cajun seasoning, paprika, and black pepper.

3. Stir well to combine, ensuring that the chicken is evenly coated with the seasonings and paprika.

4. In a large frying pan or skillet, over moderate heat, add the olive oil and fry the chicken while gradually, add ¼ cup of the chicken broth.

5. When the chicken is sufficiently cooked and its juice run clear, set to one side.

6. In the frying pan, melt the butter and stir in the flour to form a roux.

7. Add, the remaining broth along with the heavy cream, whisking slowly to incorporate.

8. Bring to boil and remove the skillet from the heat.

9. Whisk in the mozzarella cheese and heavy cream and add a splash of Tabasco.

10. Add the spaghetti and toss to combine.

11. Serve hot and top with the cooked chicken.

Recipe 17: Nonna's Traditional Spaghetti Bolognese

Nonna's authentic recipe for a traditional and classic Bolognese – this, she says is how it should be prepared!

Yield: 2-4

Preparation Time: **5mins**

Cook Time: 1hour 45mins

Preparation Time:**1hour 50mins**

Ingredient List:
- 2 tablespoons olive oil
- 6 rashers streaky pancetta (chopped)
- 2 large onions (chopped)
- 3 cloves garlic (peeled, crushed)
- 1 pound lean, best minced beef

- ¾ cup red wine
- 2 (14 ounce) can chopped tomatoes
- 2 medium carrots (chopped)
- 1 stick celery (chopped)
- 2 fresh bay leaves
- 2 pounds dried spaghetti or tagliatelle
- Salt
- Parmesan cheese (fresh grated, to serve)
- Freshly ground black pepper

Instructions:

1. In a large heavy pan, heat the olive oil, add the pancetta and fry over moderate heat, until golden.

2. Add the onions along with the crushed garlic, and sauté until just softened.

3. Increase the temperature and add the beef to the pan, frying until browned.

4. Pour in the red wine and boil until the liquid reduces by approximately a 1/3.

5. Reduce the heat, and stir in the canned tomatoes, carrots, celery and bay leaves.

6. Cover the pot with a tight-fitting lid and over a gentle heat; simmer for 1 -1½ hours until the sauce is thickened and rich, occasionally stirring.

7. Boil the spaghetti in plenty of salted water. Drain and divide between bowls.

8. Scatter a little Parmesan over the spaghetti and top with a generous ladleful of Bolognese sauce.

9. Garnish with more Parmesan and a dash of freshly ground pepper.

Recipe 18: Corsican Spaghetti

Corsican cuisine is steeped in tradition with many recipes being passed from one generation to the next.

Yield: 2

Preparation Time: **10mins**

Cook Time: **55mins**

Total Cooking Time: **1hour 5mins**

Ingredient List:
- 2 ounces butter (divided)
- 1 yellow onion (peeled, finely chopped)
- 1 clove garlic (peeled, crushed)
- ½ pound good quality minced beef
- 8 ounces ripe tomatoes, (blanched, peeled, coarsely chopped)
- 1 small dried chili
- Salt
- 8 ounces uncooked spaghetti

- 6 green olives (pitted)
- Black pepper
- 1 ounce Parmesan cheese (grated)

Instructions:

1. In a saucepan over moderate heat, melt 1 ounce of butter, add the onion and sauté until just browned.

2. Add the garlic, minced beef, chopped tomatoes, chili and salt and simmer for 45 minutes.

3. In a large pot of salted boiling water, cook the spaghetti according to the package instructions. Drain and add the remaining butter, allowing it to melt.

4. Remove the chili from the sauce.

5. Add the olives to the sauce, taste and season as necessary.

6. Heap the spaghetti into a warm serving bowl and pour the sauce over the top.

7. Serve the grated cheese on the side.

Recipe 19: Fresh Pasta With Lamb And Bell Pepper Sauce

Spaghetti alla Chitarra con Ragù di Agnello e Peperoni is an elegant more sophisticated traditional pasta dish from the Abruzzo region of Italy.

Yield: 2

Preparation Time: **30mins**

Cook Time: 2hours 25mins

Total Cooking Time: **2hours 55mins**

Ingredient List:
- 2 tablespoons virgin olive oil
- 1 whole clove garlic (peeled)
- 1 fresh bay leaf
- ½ pound minced lamb
- 3 red bell peppers (seeded, cut into strips)
- 3 yellow bell peppers (seeded, cut into strips)

- ⅓ cup dry white Italian wine
- 1 pound plum tomatoes (peeled, seeded, diced)
- 4 tablespoons strong concentrated lamb stock
- Salt
- Freshly ground black pepper

For the pasta:

- 2 medium eggs
- 1¼ cups semola di grano duro rimacinata (re-milled durum flour)
- Parmigiano Regina (freshly grated)

Instructions:

1. In a large frying pan over medium heat, heat the olive oil. Add the whole clove of peeled garlic along with the bay leaf and fry until the garlic emits its fragrance.

2. Add the minced lamb and over moderate heat, gently brown.

3. Next, add the red and yellow pepper strips and sauté for 60 seconds.

4. Pour in the wine and cook, while stirring, until the majority of the wine evaporates.

5. Add the chopped tomatoes, along with the lamb stock. Stir to combine, lower the temperature while

allowing to simmer, occasionally stirring. Season to taste.

6. To prepare the pasta: In a bowl, combine the eggs with the flour, and set to one side for 30 minutes.

7. Roll the dough out to a thickness of around ½" and cut into ½" wide noodles.

8. Lay the spaghetti on a clean and lightly floured work surface; this will prevent them from sticking together.

9. The ragu is cooked once the sauce has sufficiently thickened; this will take between 1- 1½ hours.

10. Remove the clove of garlic along with the bay leaf.

11. To a large pot of boiling, salted water, add the spaghetti and cook for 6-8 minutes until the spaghetti has a bite (al dente).

12. Using a colander, drain the spaghetti, setting a small amount of cooking water to one side, add the pasta to the ragu.

13. Toss well to combine, adding a drop of cooking water if necessary.

14. Divide between pasta bowls, and garnish with grated cheese.

Recipe 20: Eggplant And Country Ham Ragù

Ragu is a meat-based sauce, usually served with pasta.

It was created in the 18th century by Alberto Alvisi.

Yield: 4

Preparation Time: **25mins**

Cook Time: 1hour 25mins

Total Cooking Time: **1hour 50mins**

Ingredient List:
- 8 tablespoons olive oil (divided)
- 1½ pounds eggplants (cut into ½ "pieces)
- Kosher salt
- Freshly ground black pepper
- 3 ounces prosciutto
- 1 medium onion (peeled and finely chopped)

- 2 medium garlic cloves (finely chopped)
- 1 canned chipotle chilies in adobo (finely chopped)
- 1 tablespoon tomato paste
- 1 tablespoon unsweetened cocoa powder
- ½ cup ready-made tomato sauce
- 1 tablespoon fish sauce
- 12 ounces spaghetti
- 2 tablespoons unsalted butter
- ½ cup Parmesan cheese (finely grated)
- 3 tablespoons parsley (finely chopped)

Instructions:

1. In a saucepan over moderate to high heat, heat 3 tablespoons of olive oil.

2. Add ¾ of the eggplant, and season with freshly ground black pepper and salt, and cook, while stirring until just tender and lightly browned, around 5-8 minutes.

3. Transfer the mixture to a medium-sized bowl and repeat the cooking process with 3 tablespoons of oil and the remaining ¾ cup of eggplant.

4. Heat 2 tablespoons of oil, over a moderate heat in the same pan, and add the prosciutto, onion, and

garlic. Cook, while occasionally stirring, until the onions become translucent and softened; about 5 minutes.

5. Add the chilies along with the tomato paste and cocoa powder, stirring well to ensure an even coating. Continue cooking while frequently stirring, until the tomato paste is a dark brick-like red and the cocoa powder emits a toasty aroma, around 2-4 minutes.

6. Add the tomato sauce together with the eggplant set aside earlier and 1 cup of water; scrape up any bits that are nicely browned.

7. Reduce the temperature to moderate to low heat and cook, occasionally stirring, until the sauce has thickened and the flavors combined, 25-30 minutes.

8. Add the fish sauce and season well.

9. In the meantime, cook the spaghetti in a large pan of boiling, salted water, for 6-8 minutes or until cooked with a bite (al dente).

10. Drain, the pasta and reserve 2 cups of cooking water.

11. Add the spaghetti to the pot with the sauce along with the butter and 1 cup of cooking water. Bring to a gentle simmer and cook, frequently tossing, until a glossy and thick sauce forms and coats the spaghetti; adding additional cooking water if necessary.

12. Divide the pasta between individual bowls and scatter with Parmesan and chopped parsley.

Chapter 3: Vegetarian Pasta

Recipe 21: Spring Vegetable Alfredo

Alfredo sauce is a heavenly combination of cream, Parmesan and a little lemon zest for freshness. A combination of green spring vegetables prevents this dish from being too heavy.

Yield: 4

Preparation Time: 5mins

Cook Time: **15mins**

Total Cooking Time: **20mins**

Ingredient List:
- Salt
- 9 ounces fresh spaghetti

- Olive oil
- ½ cup unsalted butter
- 4 ounces shiitake mushrooms (stems discarded, caps sliced ¼" thick)
- 1 pound thin-stemmed asparagus
- ½ cup frozen snow peas
- Black pepper
- 2 cups heavy cream
- 1½ cups Parmigiano Reggiano
- Zest ½ a lemon (grated)
- 1 tablespoon fresh chives (chopped)

Instructions:

1. In a deep pot of well-salted boiling water, add the fresh spaghetti. Cook according to package instructions. Set aside ½ a cup of the cooking water.

2. Drain the cooked spaghetti in a colander and toss with a drop of oil.

3. In a heavy skillet melt 2 tablespoons of butter on moderate heat. Arrange the mushrooms in the skillet in a single layer. Sauté for a couple of minutes without stirring, then stir quickly and cook for another couple of minutes.

4. Add in the asparagus along with another tablespoon of butter a generous pinch of salt. Cook for 3-5 minutes. Toss the cooked vegetables in the colander with the spaghetti.

5. Melt the remaining butter in the skillet and whisk in the cream. Cook until simmering then toss in the peas. Cook for a couple of minutes before taking off the heat.

6. Sprinkle the cheese into the sauce and stir to combine.

7. Add the pasta and vegetables to the sauce along with the lemon zest and chives. Toss until the spaghetti is coated in the sauce. Taste and season as needed.

8. Serve immediately.

Recipe 22: Cacio E Pepe

This pasta dish is Roman, and the name literally translates as cheese and pepper. It's a simple recipe with only four main ingredients, and the secret of this dish lies in the sauce.

Yield: 2

Preparation Time: **10mins**

Cook Time: **18mins**

Total Cooking Time: **30mins**

Ingredient List:
- Kosher salt
- 6 ounces uncooked spaghetti
- 3 tablespoons unsalted butter (chilled, cubed)
- 1 teaspoon freshly cracked black pepper
- ¾ cup Grana Padano (finely grated)
- ⅓ cup Pecorino (finely grated)

Instructions:

1. In a large pot (between 5-6 quarts) bring 3 quarts of cold water to a boil.

2. Season with kosher salt and add the uncooked spaghetti, and cook occasionally stirring, until a couple of minutes before it becomes tender. Drain the pasta, and set ¾ of a cup of cooking water aside.

3. In the meantime, in a large frying pan or skillet over moderate heat, melt the unsalted butter.

4. Add the black pepper and cook, while swirling the skillet, until toasted, for around 60 seconds.

5. Pour ½ cup of the pasta cooking water to the skillet and bring to a gentle simmer.

6. Add the pasta along with the remaining butter.

7. Reduce to a low heat, and add the finely grated Grana Padano, stirring and using tongs to toss, until the cheese melts.

8. Remove from the heat, add the Pecorino, and stirring, and using kitchen tongs to toss, until the

cheese melts and sauce totally covers the pasta and the pasta is al dente.

9. Add additional water if needed.

10. Transfer the spaghetti to individual bowls and enjoy.

Recipe 23: Spanish Spaghetti

Toasted almonds provide flavor and texture, giving each mouthful a delightful and delicate crunch.

Yield: 4

Preparation Time: **5mins**

Cook Time: **15mins**

Total Cooking Time: **20mins**

Ingredient List:

- Salt
- 1 pound uncooked spaghetti
- ¼ cup good quality olive oil
- 3 teaspoons anchovy paste
- 4 garlic cloves (finely chopped)
- 4 roasted red peppers
- Black pepper
- 1 cup black olives (pitted, finely chopped)
- ½ cup slivered almonds (toasted)

Instructions:

1. Salt a large pan of boiling water, cook the spaghetti in it until 1-2 minutes away from being done. Set aside a ladleful of the cooking water.

2. Over moderate heat, warm the oil in a heavy skillet.

3. Add the anchovy paste and garlic to the skillet, sauté for 5-6 minutes.

4. Add the roasted peppers into a food processor and then blitz to a paste. Add the pepper paste the skillet. Stir well and season a little with little black pepper.

5. Stir in the reserved pasta water and cooked spaghetti to the skillet, tossing to coat it in the sauce.

6. Stir in the olives and almonds.

7. Serve immediately.

Recipe 24: Caprese Spaghetti

Serve as a side dish, appetizer or light lunch.

Yield: 2-3

Preparation Time: **10mins**

Cook Time: **30mins**

Total Cooking Time: **40mins**

Ingredient List:
- 10 ounces uncooked spaghetti
- ¼ cup virgin olive oil
- 4 cloves garlic (peeled, finely chopped)
- 2 cups cherry tomatoes (halved)
- 1 teaspoon kosher salt
- ½ pound fresh mozzarella (cut into small cubes)
- 8 large basil leaves (torn)

Instructions:

1. Cook the pasta according to the manufacturer's instructions and set to one side.

2. In a pan, over moderate heat, heat the oil, and sauté the garlic until it just begins to turn brown. Stir in the cherry tomatoes and salt and toss them in the olive oil and garlic.

3. Cook the tomatoes, until they are soft and beginning to burst, 12-15 minutes.

4. Add the tomatoes and the oil to the spaghetti, along with the mozzarella. Scatter with torn basil and serve warm.

Recipe 25: Spaghetti In A Blush Sauce

Super tomatoey, super creamy, and super fabulous.

Yield: 4

Preparation Time: **5mins**

Cook Time: **20mins**

Total Cooking Time: **25mins**

Ingredient List:

- 12 ounces uncooked spaghetti
- 2 tablespoons virgin olive oil
- 4 cloves garlic (minced)
- 2 (14 ounces) canned strained tomatoes
- Salt and pepper
- ½ teaspoons crushed chili flakes
- ½ cup white wine
- 1 small onion (chopped)
- ¾ cup half and half
- Basil (to garnish)

- Parmesan cheese (freshly grated)

Instructions:

1. Cook the spaghetti according to the package instructions.

2. In a large skillet or frying pan, heat the oil, over moderate heat.

3. Add the minced garlic along with the canned tomatoes and cook for 2-3 minutes.

4. Next, add the seasoning, crushed chili flakes, and white wine, bring to a simmer, cover with a lid and cook, while stirring, for 8-10 minutes, or until the sauce thickens.

5. Pour in the half and half and then cook until the mixture starts to bubble, stirring well to combine.

6. Add the cooked pasta to the pan, and toss to combine.

7. Cook for 2-3 minutes more or until the sauce is thickened and the pasta, evenly coated.

8. Serve garnished with chopped basil.

9. Sprinkle with grated Parmesan.

Recipe 26: Chocolate Spaghetti

Love it or hate it, but you gotta try it; spaghetti in a dark chocolate sauce is the height of decadence!

Yield: 2-4

Preparation Time: 4mins

Cook Time: **5mins**

Total Cooking Time: **9mins**

Ingredient List:
- 2 tablespoons butter
- 4 ounces cream cheese
- ½ cup powdered sugar
- ¼ cup heavy cream
- 1 cup dark chocolate chips + more for garnish
- 8 ounces cooked spaghetti

Instructions:

1. In a saucepan over moderate heat, heat the butter along with the cream cheese.

2. Add the powdered sugar, whisking to combine along with the heavy cream.

3. Next, whisk in the dark chocolate chips until the chocolate sauce is silky smooth.

4. Add the cooked spaghetti to the pan and combine to ensure that it is evenly coated in the chocolate sauce.

5. Sprinkle with additional chocolate chips.

Recipe 27: Spaghetti With Four Cheeses

Curl up on the sofa this National Spaghetti Day with a big bowl of ooey, gooey, cheesy spaghetti – the very best in comfort food.

Yield: 4

Preparation Time: **10mins**

Cook Time: **25mins**

Total Cooking Time: 35mins

Ingredient List:
- 8 ounces uncooked spaghetti
- 1 tablespoon olive oil
- 1 tablespoon butter
- 5 cloves garlic (minced)
- 1 chicken bouillon cube
- 1 cup heavy cream
- 1 cup Fontina cheese (shredded)

- ½ Provolone cheese (grated)
- ¼ cup Parmesan cheese (grated)
- 2 tablespoons parsley (chopped)

Instructions:

1. First prepare the spaghetti according to the package directions, Drain and keep hot. Reserving a cup of cooking water.

2. In the meantime, in a saucepan over moderate heat, heat the olive oil along with the butter.

3. Add the garlic and cook for 60 seconds.

4. Add the pasta cooking water, chicken bouillon cube, heavy cream and cooked pasta and season.

5. Bring to the oil, while constantly stirring. As soon as the liquid comes to boil, add the Fontina, Provolone, and Parmesan cheeses and continue stirring until the ingredients are fully incorporated, for 60 seconds, or until the cheeses coat the spaghetti.

6. Reduce the heat to a simmer, and continue cooking while stirring continually, to thicken, for 1-2 minutes.

7. To serve, garnish with chopped parsley.

Recipe 28: French Spaghetti

A veggie-packed dish that is full of flavor with creamy, and indulgent cream and milk.

Yield: 4

Preparation Time: **20mins**

Cook Time: **1hour**

Total Cooking Time: **1hour 20mins**

Ingredient List:
- 8 ounces uncooked spaghetti
- 1¼ cups green peppers (chopped)
- ⅔ cup onion (peeled, chopped)
- 2 tablespoons butter
- 1 (14½ ounce) canned diced tomatoes
- 1 (4 ounce) canned, sliced mushrooms (drained)
- ¼ cup ripe olives (drained, pitted, sliced)
- 1 tablespoon butter
- 4 teaspoons all-purpose flour

- ⅛ teaspoons salt
- ¾ cup whipping cream
- ¾ cup whole milk
- ¼ cup Parmesan (grated)

Instructions:

1. First, cook the spaghetti according to the package instructions and drain.

2. In a frying pan, cook the peppers along with the onions in 2 tablespoons butter, until the veggies are tender.

3. Add the tomatoes (un-drained) and bring to boil. Reduce the heat to a simmer, uncovered for 15 minutes. Add the mushrooms and slices of olives, and stir to combine.

4. In the meantime, make the white sauce: In a medium-sized pan, melt 1 tablespoon of butter.

5. Stir in the flour and salt, and add the whipping cream followed immediately by the whole milk.

6. Cook while stirring until the mixture is bubbly and thickened. Remove the pan from the heat.

7. Arrange the cooked pasta in an 8x8x2" baking dish and top with the white sauce, followed by the tomato and mushroom sauce.

8. Scatter Parmesan cheese over the top.

9. Bake in the oven, with no lid, at a temperature of 350 degrees F until heated through, 20-25 minutes.

10. Serve warm.

Recipe 29: Spaghetti With Artichokes, Pine Nuts, And Pesto

A flavorsome spaghetti dish to serve as a dinner party appetizer.

Yield: 4

Preparation Time: **5mins**

Cook Time: **15mins**

Total Cooking Time: **20mins**

Ingredient List:

- 12 ounces uncooked spaghetti
- 2 medium eggs
- 2 tablespoons whole milk
- 4 tablespoons green pesto
- 4 tablespoons Parmesan (cheese)
- 1 (13.75 ounce) can artichoke (drained, quartered, dried)

- Salt and pepper
- 3 tablespoons pine nuts

Instructions:

1. Cook the spaghetti following package directions.

2. In the meantime, in a small mixing bowl, beat both of the eggs together with the whole milk, green pesto, Parmesan, artichokes, and seasoning.

3. Heat a frying pan over moderate heat, and add the pine nuts, toasting for 2-3 minutes, shaking and swirling the pan once or twice, until they are a light golden color. Take care not to burn.

4. Drain the spaghetti in a colander and tip it back into the pan. Set the pan over low heat and pour over egg mixture, tossing well to evenly coat the spaghetti, but without scrambling the eggs.

5. Toss in the pine nuts and scatter with addition grated Parmesan.

Recipe 30: Morel And Asparagus Spaghetti

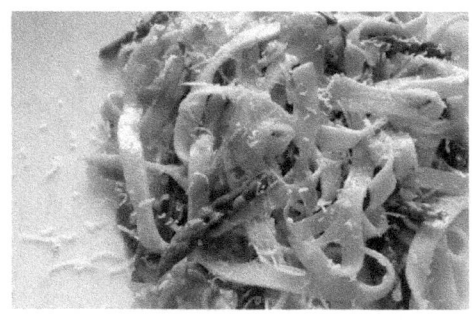

Earthy mushrooms and fresh asparagus combine perfectly with a rich, creamy sauce.

Yield: 4

Preparation Time: **20mins**

Cook Time: **20mins**

Total Cooking Time: **40mins**

Ingredient List:

- 8 cups boiling water
- 6 dried morel mushrooms
- 1 pound uncooked spaghetti
- Salt
- 3 tablespoons unsalted butter
- ¼ cup olive oil (plus more to drizzle)
- 6 cloves garlic (thinly sliced)
- 3 medium shallots (finely chopped)

- 1 pound asparagus (ends trimmed, cut into 1" pieces)
- ¾ cup vegetable stock
- ½ cup heavy cream
- Juice and zest of 1 lemon
- Kosher salt
- Black pepper
- ¼ cup Parmesan cheese (grated)

Instructions:

1. Add 8 cups of boiling water to a mixing bowl. Add the morels and set to one side, for around half an hour, or until the morels are just tender.

2. Using a slotted kitchen utensil, transfer the morels to a chopping board and cut in half across their length.

3. Pour the water used to soak the morels, in a large pan, discarding any sediment or dirt.

4. Add more water as needed to cook the spaghetti and bring to boil. Season the water with salt, add the pasta, cook, while stirring, until the pasta is al dente, around 9-12 minutes.

5. In the meantime, heat the butter along with the oil over moderate to high heat. Add the garlic together

with the shallots, and cook, occasionally stirring, until golden, approximately 3-4 minutes.

6. Add the morels, along with the asparagus and vegetable stock, bring to a rapid boil.

7. Cook, with no lid, until the asparagus is just tender, approximately 4 minutes. Remove the lid, add the heavy cream and cook until the mixture slightly reduces; about 2-3 minutes.

8. Remove from the heat, and add the spaghetti, lemon zest, salt, pepper, and Parmesan. Toss until incorporated.

9. Drizzle a little oil and scatter with more Parmesan.

Recipe 31: Spaghetti Salad

Feed a crowd with this flavorsome salad.

Yield: 15

Preparation Time: **20mins**

Cook Time: **10mins**

Total Cooking Time: **30mins**

Ingredient List:

- 1 pound spaghetti (broken in 3½" pieces)
- 3 Roma tomatoes (chopped finely)
- 1 medium zucchini (chopped finely)
- 1 medium yellow zucchini squash (chopped finely)
- 2 bell peppers (1 red, 1 green, chopped finely)
- 1 large red onion (chopped finely)
- 1 large cucumber (chopped finely)
- 2 (2.25 ounce) cans sliced olives (drained)
- 8 ounces Cheddar cheese (cubed)

Dressing:

- 1 (16 ounce) bottle Italian dressing
- ¼ cup Parmesan cheese (freshly grated)
- 1 teaspoon paprika
- ¼ teaspoons garlic powder

Instructions:

1. Cook the pasta according to package instructions and then rinse in cold water. Using a colander, drain and set to one side.

2. In a large bowl, combine the tomatoes, zucchini, squash, green peppers, red peppers, onion, cucumber, olives and Cheddar cheese. Add the cold spaghetti and stir to combine.

3. In a small mixing bowl, add the Italian dressing to the Parmesan, paprika, and garlic powder.

4. Pour the dressing on top of the pasta and the veggies and mix until totally incorporated.

5. Transfer the spaghetti salad to the refrigerator for 2-3 hours to chill; this always enables the flavors to intensify.

Recipe 32: Red Pesto Spaghetti

Homemade sun-dried tomato pesto is a delicious but super quick dish. Ideal for midweek dinner.

Yield: 4

Preparation Time: **10mins**

Cook Time: **18mins**

Total Cooking Time: **30mins**

Ingredient List:
- 5 ounces sun-dried tomatoes
- 1 clove garlic
- 2 tablespoons pine nuts (toasted)
- ½ teaspoons chili flakes
- 5 tablespoons good quality olive oil
- 2 teaspoons balsamic vinegar
- Salt and pepper
- 1 pound uncooked spaghetti
- Few fresh leaves of basil

Instructions:

1. In a food processor, add the sun-dried tomatoes, garlic pine nuts, chili flakes and olive oil. Blitz until you have a smooth paste.

2. Stir in the balsamic and season with salt and pepper as needed.

3. Cook the spaghetti in a pot of boiling water, according to package instruction. Drain the pasta using a colander, reserving a little of the cooking water.

4. Return the pasta to the pot along with the pesto.

5. Toss to coat the spaghetti evenly and heat until hot through. Add a drop of the reserved cooking water if it looks a little dry.

6. Serve with a garnish of fresh basil.

Recipe 33: Spaghetti Primavera

A healthy spaghetti dish that combines eggplants with lots of fresh veggies.

Yield: 4

Preparation Time: **20mints**

Cook Time: **20mins**

Total Cooking Time: **40mins**

Ingredient List:
- 1 pound eggplant (trimmed, diced)
- ½ teaspoons salt (for eggplant)
- 12 ounces uncooked spaghetti
- 1 cup water
- ½ pound green beans (trimmed)
- 1 stalk broccoli (cut into small florets)
- ¼ cup olive oil
- 1 medium zucchini (quartered lengthwise and sliced ½" thick crosswise)

- 1 red bell pepper (halved, cut into strips)
- 1 yellow bell pepper (halved, cut into strips)
- 2 cloves garlic (peeled, smashed)
- 2 cups tomato sauce
- ½ cup vegetable broth
- Freshly ground black pepper
- Parmesan (grated, to garnish)

Instructions:

1. Add half of the eggplant to a colander, and sprinkle it with table salt, add the other half of the eggplant and sprinkle with table salt.

2. Leave the colander to stand in the kitchen sink for 10 minutes, as this will get rid of the eggplant's bitterness. (Do not rinse at this stage).

3. Cook the spaghetti, until al dente, and according to the package instructions.

4. In the meantime, in a frying pan, bring the water to boil. Add the beans along with the broccoli, and cover with a tight fitting lid over moderate heat until just tender, approximately 5-6 minutes.

5. Using a colander, drain the veggies and rinse with cold water.

6. Rinse the eggplant with cold water, and pat dry using kitchen paper towel.

7. Add 3 tablespoon of olive oil to the frying pan and place over moderate to high heat.

8. Add the eggplant and cook, while stirring, until golden, 3-4 minutes.

9. Add the remaining oil along with the zucchini, bell peppers, and garlic. Stir well and cook for 2-3 minutes.

10. Stir in the tomato sauce, and broth, bring to simmer, while occasionally stirring, until the sauce thickens and the veggies are tender, 5 minutes.

11. Add the beans along with the broccoli and heat through.

12. Drain the pasta and place it in a large bowl. Add the veggie sauce, season with black pepper and scatter grated Parmesan over the top, toss to incorporate.

Recipe 34: Red-Wine Spaghetti With Walnuts And Parsley

Flavor and texture combine to deliver a recipe that could easily take pride of place on any restaurant menu.

Yield: 4

Preparation Time: **10mins**

Cook Time: **15mins**

Total Cooking Time: **25mins**

Ingredient List:
- 5 cups water
- 3¼ cups dry red wine (divided)
- Salt
- 12 ounces uncooked spaghetti
- ¼ cup virgin olive oil (divided)
- 4 cloves garlic (peeled, thinly sliced)
- ¼ teaspoons crushed red pepper

- ½ cup parsley (finely chopped)
- 4 ounces toasted walnuts (coarsely chopped)
- ½ cup Parmigiano-Reggiano cheese (grated)
- Black pepper

Instructions:

1. In a large saucepan, combine the 5 cups of water, along with 3 cups of red wine and a generous pinch of salt and bring to boil.

2. Add the spaghetti, and cook, while stirring, until it is al dente. Drain the spaghetti, and set a ¼ cup of the pasta cooking water to one side.

3. In a frying pan or skillet, heat 2 tablespoons of the oil and add the garlic and crushed red pepper and season with salt.

4. Cook over medium heat for 60 seconds and add the remaining wine along with the pasta cooking water, and bring to simmer.

5. Add the spaghetti and cook for 2-3 minutes, or until the liquid is virtually all absorbed.

6. Add the chopped parsley along with the walnuts, Parmigiano cheese, and the remaining olive oil and toss to evenly coat.

7. Season with black pepper and serve.

Recipe 35: Spaghetti Napoli

Searching for an alternative midweek dish? A classic Italian recipe, made using tomatoes, celery, and olives. It's that simple to create a tasty and filling meal.

Yield: 4

Preparation Time: **5mins**

Cook Time: **25mins**

Total Cooking Time: **30mins**

Ingredient List:
- 14 ounces uncooked spaghetti
- 3 tablespoons virgin olive oil
- 1 onion (peeled, chopped)
- 2 medium garlic cloves (peeled, chopped)
- 1 stick celery chopped)
- 7 tablespoons Chianti
- 1 (14 ounce) can chopped tomatoes

- 3½ ounces black olives (pitted)
- ½ teaspoons sugar
- Salt
- Black pepper
- 2 tablespoons basil (chopped)

Instructions:

1. Cook the pasta according to the package instructions, using a colander drain and set to one side.

2. In a frying pan, heat the oil and sauté the onions until softened.

3. Add the chopped garlic and cook for 60 seconds, then add the chopped celery and cook for 5 minutes. Next, add the Chianti.

4. Let the red wine bubble for 60 seconds before adding the chopped tomatoes; cooking for another 15 minutes, while occasionally stirring.

5. Add the black olives together with the sugar, taste and season.

6. Stir the sauce into the drained spaghetti and serve garnished with chopped basil.

7. Enjoy.

Recipe 36: Ricotta Spaghetti

This wonderful pasta is made with nothing more than ricotta, fresh basil, and garlic.

Yield: 6

Preparation Time: **10mins**

Cook Time: **15mins**

Total Cooking Time: **25mins**

Ingredient List:
- Salt
- ¾ pound spaghetti
- 1 garlic clove (minced)
- 1 cup part-skim ricotta cheese
- 2 teaspoons fresh basil (chopped)
- Black pepper
- 2 tablespoons Parmesan cheese (grated)

Instructions:

1. Fill a large pan with water, and lightly salt, over high heat, bring to a rolling boil.

2. Add the spaghetti, stir and return to a boil.

3. Cook the spaghetti, occasionally stirring, until cooked through but al dente, between 10-12 minutes.

4. Using a colander, drain the pasta over the kitchen sink, setting 2 tablespoons of the pasta cooking water to one side.

5. Add the minced garlic, ricotta cheese, and basil to a pan over moderate to low heat; stir until hot for approximately 4 minutes.

6. Season well and stir in the salt and black pepper, add the pasta along with the reserved cooking water.

7. Scatter grated Parmesan over the top and serve.

Recipe 37: Spaghetti Genovese

Traditionally this particular recipe consists of spaghetti, pesto, green beans, and potatoes. However, we have given this a superfood boost by combining spinach with fiber-rich whole-wheat spaghetti.

Yield:

Preparation Time: **15mins**

Cook Time: **25mins**

Total Cooking Time: **40mins**

Ingredient List:
- 2 cups packed baby spinach
- 8 ounces whole-wheat spaghetti
- 4 ounces new potatoes (thinly sliced)
- 1 pound green beans (trimmed, cut into 1" pieces)
- ½ cup prepared pesto

- 1 teaspoon freshly ground pepper

Instructions:

1. Over moderate to high heat, bring a pan of water to boil.

2. Add the baby spinach and continue cooking until wilted, around 40-45 seconds.

3. Using a slotted spoon transfer the spinach to a food blender.

Bring the water back to boil and add the whole-wheat spaghetti along with the potatoes.

4. Cook, while stirring a couple of times, until nearly tender, 6-8 minutes.

5. Add the green beans and cook for 3-4 minutes, or until just tender.

6. When the spaghetti and veggies are nearly done, carefully scoop out 1 cup of cooking water from the pan.

7. Pour half of the cooking water into the food blender, and add the pesto together with the salt and pepper.

Blitz until silky, scraping down the sides of the blender as needed.

8. Using a colander, drain the spaghetti and veggies and return them to the pan, add the pesto mixture, stirring to combine.

9. Cook over moderate heat, while gently stirring, until the sauce thickens and the spaghetti is hot, 1-2 minutes.

10. Add additional cooking water, as needed.

Recipe 38: Rocket Spaghetti

A warm arugula and spaghetti salad, perfect as a side, snack or an appetizer.

Yield: 4

Preparation Time: **8mins**

Cook Time: **12mins**

Total Cooking Time: **20mins**

Ingredient List:

- 14 ounces uncooked spaghetti
- 2½ cups fresh arugula
- 3 tablespoons olive oil
- 1 clove garlic (peeled, fine chopped)
- Salt
- Black pepper
- Arugula leaves (chopped, to garnish)

- Parmesan (freshly grated)

Instructions:

1. Cook the spaghetti, until al dente, according to the package directions. Drain, and keep warm. Reserve 1 cup of pasta cooking water.

2. Wash and sort the arugula, shaking dry to remove any water. Chop roughly, holding a couple of leaves back for garnish.

3. In a frying pan, heat the olive oil, and sweat the chopped garlic until it is translucent.

4. Add 1 ladleful of the pasta cooking water.

5. Add the pasta to the frying pan, and mix to combine.

6. Add the arugula and season well.

7. Serve with arugula leaves to garnish and sprinkle freshly grated Parmesan over the top.

Recipe 39: Spaghetti Aglio E Olio

This dish is quick and simple to make, and what's more, it used ingredients that are more than likely lying around your kitchen cupboards.

Yield: 4

Preparation Time: **2mins**

Cook Time: **8mins**

Total Cooking Time: 10mins.

Ingredient List:
- Salt
- 1 pound uncooked spaghetti
- ¼ cup virgin olive oil
- 1 teaspoon crushed red pepper flakes
- 6 garlic cloves (finely chopped)
- 1 tablespoon salted butter
- ½ teaspoons kosher salt

- ½ cup parsley (finely chopped)
- 1 cup Parmesan cheese (freshly grated)

Instructions:

1. Bring a deep pot of salted water to the boil. Add the spaghetti and cook according to the package instructions.

2. In the meantime, in a frying pan over moderate heat, heat the oil.

3. Add the pepper flakes and garlic to the frying pan and cook until the garlic becomes golden, taking great care not to overcook as this can make the garlic taste bitter. Remove from the heat and add the butter, stirring to combine.

4. Drain the spaghetti, and set one cup of pasta cooking water aside.

5. Add the drained spaghetti to the frying pan and toss to evenly coat.

6. Increase the heat to moderate to high and add the pasta cooking water. Stir.

7. Bring the mixture to boil, reduce the heat and add the salt.

8. Continue cooking until the mixture reduces by approximately half.

9. Turn the heat off and toss the spaghetti with the chopped parsley and grated cheese.

10. Serve and enjoy.

Recipe 40: Spaghetti Alla Vesuviana

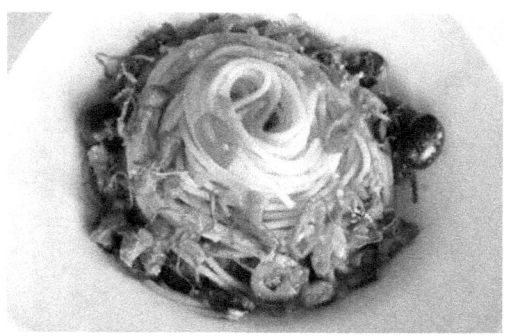

A dish from Naples, home of the pizza, made with spaghetti, in a rich tomato sauce, including Italian olives, chili, and seasoning.

Yield: 4-6

Preparation Time: **5mins**

Cook Time: **15mins**

Total Cooking Time:**20mins**

Ingredient List:
- 3 tablespoons extra virgin olive oil
- 2 cloves garlic (thinly sliced)
- 7 large, ripe Roma tomatoes (chopped)
- 3 tablespoons tiny (nonpareil) capers
- ⅓ Italian green olives (pitted, chopped)
- 1 teaspoon fresh red finger chili (minced)
- 1 tablespoon Kosher salt

- 1 pound uncooked spaghetti
- 2 tablespoons Italian parsley leaves (chopped)
- 3 tablespoons Parmigiano-Reggiano (freshly grated)

Instructions:

1. In a pasta pot, with lid, over a high heat, bring cold water to a fast boil.

2. In the meantime, in a large frying pan, over moderate to high heat, heat the olive oil.

3. Add the garlic and sauté, while stirring, for 1-2 minutes, or until translucent but not browned.

4. Add the tomatoes, along with the capers, chopped green olives, and red finger chili, and reduce the heat to moderate. Allow to simmer until the spaghetti is cooked.

5. In the meantime, and while the sauce simmers, add the salt and spaghetti to the boiling water in the pasta pot, and cook, over high heat, uncovered, until the spaghetti is al dente. Take a scoop, and remove approximately 1 cup of the pasta cooking water for the pot, and set to one side. Using a colander drain the spaghetti.

6. Add 2 tablespoons of the pasta cooking water to the tomato mixture and increase to high heat.

7. Add the drained spaghetti and toss well to evenly coat. Add a drop more pasta cooking water if you feel the mixture is too dry.

8. Add the chopped parsley along with the Parmigiano and toss to coat.

9. Serve.

Part 2

Making Your Own Homemade Pasta

When it comes to making your own homemade pasta, having the right pasta machine is essential. Pasta makers come in all different shapes and sizes and can be manual or automatic. The manual pasta makers are the authentic, original machines. Now of days they are making electric pasta machines, which takes a little away from how authentic the hole process is.

When looking for the right machine for your home and restaurant, which one is right for you? Whether your getting one for your home, or for a restaurant, will pretty much be the biggest decision you'll have to make. If your getting one for your home, the machine will only need to be small, just big enough to make enough pasta for your family, or a small group of people.

If you own a restaurant and want a highly efficient pasta maker, then getting a bigger, faster, or maybe even an electric pasta machine would be a good idea. When dealing with a restaurant, the speed, amount made, and quality is the key to success.

There are many pasta cutters out there that work fantastic, and will get the trick done. But then there's ones that are high in quality, and will last you forever. When it comes to deciding on the right one to purchase, take quality, durability, and efficiency into consideration. I like to read reviews on the machines before I purchase one. Seeing what other buyers have to say is very helpful when making a decision on purchasing something.

If your thinking about getting into making your own homemade noodles for your pasta, then getting a pasta machine is the right idea. Go out and grab a nice, affordable, quality pasta machine for your home or restaurant, you wont regret it!

Getting a pasta maker was a great decision for my household. My grandmother just moved in and loves to cook just as much, if not more than my mother. My family is from Italy and we love a good sauce. Every Sunday we break out all the ingredients, the pasta makers, and everything we need to make our homemade pasta.

My friends come over every once in a while and say my mother has the best sauce out there! And to top it off the noodles are homemade right in my kitchen from our new pasta cutter. When it comes to a good homemade pasta, nothing beats the homemade noodles, with the homemade sauce and meatballs to go with it. Little bit of Parmesan cheese, and your ready to go!

Egg Noodles

Prep Time : 15 Minutes

Cook Time : 3 Minutes

Ready In : 33 Minutes

Servings : 7

"Delectable home-made egg noodles are a simple matter of flour, salt, eggs, milk and butter kneaded into a dough, rolled out and cut into shapes. Hint: dry the pasta for 20 minutes before cutting, then dry the cut shapes until no longer moist and sticky."

INGREDIENTS:

2 1/2 cups all-purpose flour

1 pinch salt

2 eggs, beaten

1/2 cup milk

1 tablespoon butter

DIRECTIONS:

1. In a large bowl, stir together the flour and salt. Add the beaten egg, milk, and butter. Knead dough until

smooth, about 5 minutes. Let rest in a covered bowl for 10 minutes.

2. On a floured surface, roll out to 1/8 or 1/4 inch thickness. Cut into desired lengths and shapes.

3. Allow to air dry before cooking.

4. To cook fresh pasta, in a large pot with boiling salted water cook until al dente.

Basic Pasta

Servings : 3

"There's no taste like home-made pasta! You'll love how a simple concordance of egg, salt, flour and water yields deliciously tender pasta to use immediately or even several days later. Hint: let the pasta sheet dry for 20 minutes before cutting."

INGREDIENTS:

1 egg, beaten

1/2 teaspoon salt

1 cup all-purpose flour

2 tablespoons water

DIRECTIONS:

1. In a medium sized bowl, combine flour and salt. Make a well in the flour, add the slightly beaten egg, and mix. Mixture should form a stiff dough. If needed, stir in 1 to 2 tablespoons water.

2. On a lightly floured surface, knead dough for about 3 to 4 minutes. With a pasta machine or by hand roll dough out to desired thinness. Use machine or knife to cut into strips of desired width.

Grandma's Noodles I

Servings : 6

"Put your pasta machine to work transforming flour, eggs and salt into tender noodles fit for your favorite home-made soups."

INGREDIENTS:

4 cups all-purpose flour

4 eggs, lightly beaten

1 teaspoon salt

DIRECTIONS:

1. Put all ingredients in the pasta machine. Let dry an hour or so.

2. Add noodles to boiling chicken stock. Cook for ten to fifteen minutes.

Grandma's Noodles Ii

Servings : 4

"Here's a handy dandy do-it-yourself recipe for marvelous egg noodles fashioned from egg, salt, milk, flour and baking powder. You'll love how they taste in soups and broths!"

INGREDIENTS:

1 egg, beaten

1/2 teaspoon salt

2 tablespoons milk

1 cup sifted all-purpose flour

1/2 teaspoon baking powder (optional)

DIRECTIONS:

1. Combine egg, salt, milk. Add flour. (For thicker noodles add baking powder to flour before mixing.) Separate into two balls.
2. Roll out dough, and let stand for 20 minutes.
3. Cut into strips and spread to dry--dust with a little flour. Let dry for approximately 2 hours.

4. Drop into hot soup--cook for about 10 minutes.

Fresh Semolina And Egg Pasta

Prep Time : 30 Minutes

Cook Time : 5 Minutes

Ready In : 1 Hour 5 Minutes

Servings : 8

"Fresh pasta is literally at your fingertips as you knead together flour, salt, eggs and olive oil to make a delectable pasta dough."

INGREDIENTS:

2 cups all-purpose flour

2 cups semolina flour

1 pinch salt

6 large eggs

2 tablespoons olive oil

DIRECTIONS:

1. Thoroughly sift together all-purpose flour, semolina flour, and pinch of salt. On a clean surface, make a mountain out of flour mixture then make a deep well in center. Break the eggs into the well and add olive oil. Whisk eggs very gently with a fork, gradually

incorporating flour from the sides of the well. When mixture becomes too thick to mix with a fork, begin kneading with your hands.

2. Knead dough for 8 to 12 minutes, until it is smooth and supple. Dust dough and work surface with semolina as needed to keep dough from becoming sticky. Wrap dough tightly in plastic and allow it to rest at room temperature for 30 minutes.

3. Roll out dough with a pasta machine or a rolling pin to desired thickness. Cut into your favorite style of noodle or stuff with your favorite filling to make ravioli. Bring water to a boil in a large pot, then add 4 teaspoons salt. Cook pasta until tender but not mushy, 1 to 8 minutes depending on thickness. Drain immediately and toss with your favorite sauce.

Grandma's Butter Noodles

Prep Time : 30 Minutes

Cook Time : 10 Minutes

Ready In   : 2 Hours 10 Minutes

Servings   : 4

"This is my late mother-in-laws recipe for noodles -- her favorite for flavor and because they don't spring back when you roll them. At every family gathering she'd make the best Chicken and Noodles, dropping her prepared noodles into homemade chicken broth along with shredded cooked chicken, then serving them over mashed potatoes. I've made them many times and everyone loves them. When making multiple batches, and lacking counter space, I hang the rounds on clean plastic hangers to dry."

INGREDIENTS:

2 eggs

3 tablespoons butter, melted and cooled

1 1/4 cups all-purpose flour

1/4 teaspoon baking powder

1 teaspoon salt

DIRECTIONS:

1. In a large bowl, whisk the eggs and melted butter together with a fork. Stir in the flour, baking powder and salt until dough becomes stiff. Knead on a lightly floured surface or in the bowl for a few minutes to blend completely. Divide the dough into thirds. On a lightly floured surface, roll each piece into a sheet about 1/16 of an inch thick. Place each sheet onto a dry cloth and set aside for 30 to 45 minutes to partially dry.

2. When the noodle sheets are somewhat dry, roll up one at a time into a loose spiral and cut into strips as wide as you want using a sharp knife. Spread out the noodles to dry for about 1 hour before cooking or storing in freezer containers. To use frozen noodles, thaw in the container before using.

3. To cook the noodles, drop into rapidly boiling water or broth, and cook until tender, 7 to 10 minutes.

Homemade Four Cheese Ravioli

Prep Time   : 45 Minutes

Cook Time : 15 Minutes

Ready In   : 2 Hours

Servings   : 4

"Fresh pasta filled with ricotta cheese, cream cheese, mozzarella cheese, and provolone cheese is drizzled with marinara sauce and finished with a pesto-Alfredo cream sauce."

INGREDIENTS:
Ravioli Dough:

2 cups all-purpose flour

1 pinch salt

1 teaspoon olive oil

2 eggs

1 1/2 tablespoons water

Ravioli Filling:

1 (8 ounce) container ricotta cheese

1 (4 ounce) package cream cheese, softened

1/2 cup shredded mozzarella cheese

1/2 cup provolone cheese, shredded

1 egg

1 1/2 teaspoons dried parsley

Pesto-Alfredo Cream Sauce:

2 tablespoons olive oil

2 cloves garlic, crushed

3 tablespoons prepared basil pesto sauce

2 cups heavy cream

1/4 cup grated Parmesan cheese

1 (24 ounce) jar marinara sauce

Egg Wash:

1 egg

1 tablespoon water

DIRECTIONS:

1. Mound the flour and salt together on a work surface and form a well. Beat the teaspoon of olive oil,

2 eggs, and water in a bowl. Pour half the egg mixture into the well. Begin mixing the egg with the flour with one hand; use your other hand to keep the flour mound steady. Add the remaining egg mixture and knead to form a dough.

2. Knead the dough until smooth, 8 to 10 minutes; add more flour if the dough is too sticky. Form the dough into a ball and wrap tightly with plastic. Refrigerate for 1 hour.

3. While the dough is resting, prepare the ravioli filling. Combine the ricotta cheese, cream cheese, mozzarella cheese, provolone cheese, egg, and parsley and mix well. Set the filling aside.

4. Heat 2 tablespoons of olive oil in a skillet over medium heat. Add the crushed garlic and pesto sauce and cook for one minute. Pour in the heavy cream, raise the heat to high, and bring the sauce to a boil. Reduce the heat and simmer for 5 minutes. Add the Parmesan cheese and stir until the cheese melts. Remove the pan from the heat and keep warm.

5. Meanwhile, in a separate saucepan, warm the marinara sauce over medium-low heat.

6. Preheat an oven to 375 degrees F (190 degrees C). Beat the egg with the tablespoon of water to make the egg wash.

7. Roll out the pasta dough into thin sheets no thicker than a nickel. To assemble the ravioli, brush the egg

wash over a sheet of pasta. Drop the filling mixture on the dough by teaspoonfuls about one inch apart. Cover the filling with the top sheet of pasta, pressing out the air from around each portion of filling. Press firmly around the filling to seal. Cut into individual ravioli with a knife or pizza cutter. Seal the edges.

8. Fill a large pot with lightly salted water and bring to a rolling boil over high heat. Stir in the ravioli, and return to a boil. Cook uncovered, stirring occasionally, until the ravioli float to the top and the filling is hot, 4 to 8 minutes. Drain well.

9. Grease a baking sheet. Place the cooked ravioli on the sheet pan and bake in the preheated oven until brown, about 4 minutes.

10. To serve the ravioli, divide them among four warmed serving bowls. Drizzle the marinara sauce over the ravioli and then top with the cream sauce.

Homemade Noodles

Servings : 2

"It just takes a few minutes to make wonderful, homemade noodles. All you need is flour, egg and a pinch of salt. What a tasty addition to fresh chicken soup!"

INGREDIENTS:

1 cup all-purpose flour

1 egg

1 pinch salt

DIRECTIONS:

1. Mix all ingredients. Roll thin with flour, then roll like a jelly roll. Cut into 1/2 inch strips. Let dry.

2. Drop into hot chicken broth. Boil for 15 minutes.

Whole Wheat Pasta

Prep Time : 40 Minutes

Ready In   : 40 Minutes

Servings   : 4

"Fresh, healthy and very delish... I sometimes make this the traditional style, and when in a hurry, I throw all the ingredients into my mixer with the kneading hook."

INGREDIENTS:

1 1/2 cups all-purpose flour

1 1/2 cups whole wheat flour

1/2 teaspoon sea salt

4 eggs

2 teaspoons olive oil

DIRECTIONS:

1. Stir together the all-purpose flour, whole wheat flour and salt in a medium bowl, or on a clean board. Make a hollow in the center, and pour in the olive oil. Break eggs into it one at a time, while mixing quickly

with a fork until the dough is wet enough to come together. Knead on a lightly floured surface until the dough is stiff and elastic. Cover, and let stand for 30 minutes to relax.

2. Roll out dough by hand with a rolling pin, or use a pasta machine to achieve the desired thickness of noodles. Cut into desired width and shapes. Allow the pasta to air dry for at least 15 minutes to avoid having it clump together.

Homemade Egg Noodles

Servings : 4

"These egg noodles must be allowed to dry for a couple of hours before boiling in chicken broth. Serve alone, or in place of mashed potatoes with a turkey dinner."

INGREDIENTS:

2 cups all-purpose flour

1/4 teaspoon salt

1/4 teaspoon baking powder

4 egg yolks

DIRECTIONS:

1. Sift together the flour, salt and baking powder. Add egg yolks and mix until dry ingredients are moistened.

2. Press into a ball and cut in quarters. Roll out on floured surface 1/8 to 1/4 inch thick; cut to desired width and length. Lay on linen dish towel or wooden dowel to dry.

3. Add to broth such as chicken or turkey and cook until done.

Chicken And Spinach Ravioli

Prep Time : 1 Hour

Cook Time : 30 Minutes

Ready In : 2 Hours

Servings : 6

"A delicious combination of chicken and spinach make a wonderful Italian meal. Make sure to have plenty of freshly grated Asiago cheese to top these ravioli."

INGREDIENTS:

4 eggs, beaten

3/4 cup water

3 3/4 cups sifted all-purpose flour

1 1/2 teaspoons salt

1/2 pound ground chicken

3/4 cup chopped fresh spinach

2 tablespoons finely chopped onion

3 tablespoons melted butter

3 tablespoons freshly grated Asiago cheese

1/4 teaspoon salt

1/4 teaspoon garlic powder

1/8 teaspoon ground nutmeg

1 pinch ground black pepper to taste

1 (16 ounce) jar marinara sauce

1/4 cup freshly grated Asiago cheese for topping

DIRECTIONS:

1. In a bowl, mix the eggs, water, 2 cups flour, and salt. Gradually mix in the remaining flour until smooth. Divide dough into 2 parts. Cover, and set aside in the refrigerator 20 minutes.

2. In a skillet over medium heat, cook the ground chicken until evenly brown; drain.

3. In a food processor, mix the chicken, spinach, and onion. Transfer to a bowl, and mix with butter, 3 tablespoons Asiago cheese, salt, garlic powder, nutmeg, and pepper.

4. On a lightly floured surface, roll out each part of the dough to 1/8 inch thickness. Cut into 2 inch squares. Place about 1 teaspoon of the chicken mixture in the center of 1/2 the squares, and top with remaining squares. Seal the edges of the squares with a moistened fork to form the ravioli.

5. Bring a large pot of lightly salted water to a boil, and cook the ravioli in small batches for about 8 minutes, or until al dente. Drain, and rinse under cold water.

6. Place the marinara sauce in a saucepan, and cook until heated through. Serve ravioli topped with marinara sauce and remaining Asiago cheese.

Pumpkin Ravioli

Servings : 6

"Taste the sweet harvest flavors of autumn in a dish of ravioli. A dough fashioned from flour, salt, olive oil, eggs and tomato paste makes a flavorful pocket for a filling rich with ricotta, pumpkin and nutmeg. Serve with Pumpkin Seed Cream Sauce."

INGREDIENTS:

1 cup ricotta cheese

1/2 cup pumpkin puree

1/2 teaspoon salt

1/4 teaspoon ground nutmeg

2 cups all-purpose flour

1/2 teaspoon salt

1/4 cup tomato paste

1 tablespoon olive oil

2 eggs

2 tablespoons water

DIRECTIONS:

1. Mix the cheese, pumpkin, 1/2 teaspoon salt, and the nutmeg. Set filling aside.

2. Mix the flour, and 1/2 teaspoon salt in a large bowl; make a well in the center of the flour. Beat the tomato paste, oil, and eggs until well blended, and pour into the well in the flour. Stir with a fork, gradually bring the flour mixture to the center of the bow until the dough makes a ball. If the dough is too dry, mix in up to 2 tablespoons water.

3. Knead lightly on a floured cloth-covered surface, adding flour if dough is sticky, until smooth and elastic, about 5 minutes. Cover, and let rest for another 5 minutes. Divide the dough into 4 equal parts. Roll the dough, one part at a time, into a rectangle about 12 x 10 inches. Keep the rest of the dough covered while working.

4. Drop 2 level teaspoons filling onto half of the rectangle, about 1 1/2 inches apart in 2 rows of 4 mounds each. Moisten the edges of the dough, and the dough between the rows of pumpkin mixture with water. Fold the other half of the dough up over the pumpkin mixture, pressing the dough down around the pumpkin. Cut between the rows of filling to make ravioli; press the edges together with a fork, or cut with a pastry wheel. Seal edges well. Repeat with the remaining dough and pumpkin filling. Place ravioli on

towel. Let stand, turning once, until dry, about 30 minutes.

5. Cook ravioli in 4 quarts of boiling salted water until tender; drain carefully.

A Farewell To Basil Fettuccine

Servings : 2

"Savor summer in Italy with every delectable mouthful of homemade pasta flavored with freshly chopped basil leaves. Toss with butter or olive oil and a grating of Parmesan cheese."

INGREDIENTS:

3/4 cup chopped fresh basil

1 1/2 cups all-purpose flour

1 egg

1 teaspoon olive oil

2 tablespoons water

2 1/2 tablespoons all-purpose flour

DIRECTIONS:

1. Using a food processor, process basil leaves until chopped very fine. Add 1 1/2 cups of flour and pulse two or three times, or until combined. Add egg, 1

teaspoon oil, and the water until dough forms a ball shape. If dough seems dry, add a bit more water. Wrap dough in a piece of plastic wrap which has been coated in a few drops of olive oil. Refrigerate dough for 2 hours.

2. Remove dough from refrigerator, and cut into 6 equal size portions. Run pasta though pasta machine, or roll with rolling pin to desired thickness. Use the additional flour to coat pasta while rolling.

3. Allow pasta to dry for one hour prior to cooking.

4. Cook in a large pot of boiling water until al dente. This should take only a 3 to 5 minutes, depending on the thickness of the pasta.

Fresh Pasta

Servings : 6

"Combine flour and eggs to make a simple, rich pasta dough. Try adding snippets of fresh herbs to small batches of the dough to make flavorful variations."

INGREDIENTS:

6 cups all-purpose flour

6 eggs

DIRECTIONS:

1. Heap the flour, and make a well in it. Break the eggs into the well. Beat eggs with a fork. Stir into the flour from the bottom of the well with the fork until the dough in the center is smooth or shiny.

2. With your hands, gradually incorporate the flour from the outside of the well toward the center, kneading gently until the mass of dough comes together. Knead the dough until it is smooth and resilient. You may need to add more flour, or you may not be able to incorporate all of the flour, depending on the humidity and the size of the eggs. If the dough is sticky or extremely pliable, knead more flour into it.

3. Divide the dough into three portions, cover with plastic wrap or an overturned bowl, and allow to rest for at least 30 minutes.

4. Roll the dough out very thin on a lightly floured surface, one portion at a time. If you have a pasta machine, follow the manufacturer's instructions for rolling out the dough into sheets about 1 millimeter thick. Use as desired.

Eggless Pasta

Servings : 4

"If you have ever wanted to make your own fresh pasta, this easy recipe shows how semolina flour, salt and water are kneaded into a simple dough, then rolled and cut into shapes. Durum semolina flour may be found at specialty grocers."

INGREDIENTS:

2 cups semolina flour

1/2 teaspoon salt

1/2 cup warm water

DIRECTIONS:

1. In a large bowl, mix flour and salt. Add warm water and stir to make a stiff dough. Increase water if dough seems too dry.

2. Pat the dough into a ball and turn out onto a lightly floured surface. Knead for 10 to 15 minutes. Cover. Let dough rest for 20 minutes.

3. Roll out dough using rolling pin or pasta machine. Work with a 1/4 of the dough at one time. Keep the rest covered, to prevent from drying out. Roll by hand

to 1/16 of an inch thick. By machine, stop at the third to last setting.

4. Cut pasta into desired shapes.

5. Cook fresh noodles in boiling salted water for 3 to 5 minutes. Drain.

Granny's Homemade Noodles

Prep Time : 30 Minutes

Ready In   : 4 Hours 30 Minutes

Servings   : 6

"This simple recipe for homemade noodles requires flour, eggs, salt, baking powder, and water."

INGREDIENTS:

4 eggs

2 tablespoons water

3 cups all-purpose flour

1 teaspoon salt

1/2 teaspoon baking powder

DIRECTIONS:

1.   Beat the eggs and water together in a bowl. Sift the flour, salt, and baking powder into a separate large bowl and make a well in the center. Pour the beaten eggs into the well, then stir in the flour mixture until a soft dough forms.

2. Roll the dough into a very thin layer on a lightly-floured surface; cut into 1/2 inch strips. Allow to dry at least 4 hours before using.

Badische Schupfnudeln (Potato Noodles)

Prep Time : 30 Minutes

Cook Time : 40 Minutes

Ready In : 1 Hour 10 Minutes

Servings : 6

"Traditional of southwestern Germany, this delicious homemade potato noodle goes well with all sorts of dishes."

INGREDIENTS:

1 1/2 pounds russet potatoes

1/2 cup all-purpose flour

1 egg

1 tablespoon chopped fresh parsley

1/2 teaspoon salt

1/4 teaspoon freshly ground nutmeg

1/4 cup lard or other cooking fat

DIRECTIONS:

1. Place whole potatoes in their skins into a large pot of boiling water; boil for 25 to 30 minutes. Remove potatoes, and discard water. When cool enough to handle, peel potatoes, and place on a lightly floured surface. Mash potatoes with a rolling pin.

2. Place mashed potatoes into a large bowl. Stir in flour, egg, parsley, salt, and nutmeg. Knead well to form a smooth dough. Then roll out the dough to a thickness of about 1/2 inch. Cut flattened dough into thin strips, about 1 1/2 inches long. Gently roll out the strips, or stretch them until the ends taper. Set aside for 15 minutes.

3. In a large skillet, heat lard over medium heat. Place the potato strips into the skillet, and fry until golden brown on both sides.

Unique Spinach Noodles

Servings   : 2

"Make your own fresh, spinach-flavored pasta! Whip up a puree of garden-fresh spinach, water, egg and salt. Combine with flour to make a dough, then roll out and cut into shapes. Let it dry before cooking. Try serving with a simple, buttery sauce."

INGREDIENTS:

1 1/4 cups torn spinach leaves

2 tablespoons water

1 egg

1/2 teaspoon salt

1 1/4 cups all-purpose flour

DIRECTIONS:

1. Combine spinach and water in a saucepan. Cover, and cook till spinach is very tender. Cool slightly.

2. Place spinach and liquid in blender container. Add egg and salt. Cover, and blend till smooth. Transfer to a bowl. Add enough flour to make a stiff dough.

3. Turn dough out onto a lightly floured surface. Knead for 1 minute. Roll very thin on a floured surface.

Let rest 20 minutes. Roll up loosely. Slice 1/4 inch wide. Unroll. Cut into desired lengths. Spread out on a rack to dry for 2 hours.

Spinach, Feta, And Pine Nut Ravioli Filling

Prep Time : 1 Hour 10 Minutes

Cook Time : 5 Minutes

Ready In : 1 Hour 15 Minutes

Servings : 4

"Fill your homemade pasta with this tangy stuffing."

INGREDIENTS:

For the Filling:

1 tablespoon olive oil

1 (10 ounce) bag fresh spinach

1 cup feta cheese

1/2 cup pine nuts

To Make the Ravioli:

2 fresh pasta sheets

1 egg

1 tablespoon water

DIRECTIONS:

1. Heat the olive oil in a large skillet over medium-high heat. Cook the spinach until fully wilted, about 2 minutes. Let cool, then squeeze the spinach to remove as much liquid as you can.

2. Combine the cooked spinach, feta, and pine nuts in a blender or food processor and pulse until it is the consistency of a fine paste. Beat the egg and water together in a small bowl.

3. To assemble the ravioli, brush the egg over a sheet of pasta. Drop the filling mixture on the dough by teaspoonfuls about one inch apart. Cover the filling with the top sheet of pasta, pressing out the air from around each portion of filling. Press firmly around the filling in whatever shape you wish (circles, squares) and then cut them apart. Press the tines of a fork around the edges of the pasta to seal each raviolo.

4. Fill a large pot with lightly salted water and bring to a rolling boil over high heat. Once the water is boiling, add the ravioli, stir gently, and return to a boil. Cook uncovered until the ravioli float to the top and the filling is hot, about 3 to 5 minutes.

Smoked Salmon Ravioli

Prep Time : 40 Minutes

Cook Time : 20 Minutes

Ready In   : 1 Hour

Servings   : 8

"Sheets of fresh pasta are filled with a savory mousse of pureed smoked salmon, eggs, cream, pepper and chives. Serve over a rich and tangy pool of melted gruyere and cream, sprinkle more gruyere over the top, and finish under the broiler."

INGREDIENTS:

2 cups all-purpose flour

2 eggs, beaten

2 egg yolks

1 pound smoked salmon

2 eggs

1 cup heavy cream

2 teaspoons chopped fresh chives

1/2 teaspoon ground black pepper

1 egg, beaten

16 ounces shredded Gruyere cheese

1 cup heavy whipping cream

DIRECTIONS:

1. TO MAKE THE PASTA, place the flour in a mound on a smooth work area, creating a well in the center. Pour the 2 beaten eggs and 2 egg yolks into the well, and slowly pull the flour into the eggs until it is all incorporated. Finish kneading by hand, adding more flour if needed for a smooth consistency. Divide the pasta in half and roll out each half or feed through pasta roller until thin, number 6 setting on the machine. Roll out as many sheets of pasta as possible.

2. FOR THE SMOKED SALMON MOUSSE, puree the smoked salmon and 2 eggs together until smooth. Slowly add 1 cup heavy cream, chopped chives, and pepper. Mix thoroughly.

3. To assemble the raviolis, prepare a smooth, floured surface. Lay out the pasta and divide the smoked salmon mousse into 24 equal-sized portions and place these portions two inches apart on one sheet of pasta. Brush the beaten egg on the pasta between the mounds of salmon mousse, and cover with the other

sheet of pasta. Cut raviolis apart, and refrigerate or freeze until you are ready to use.

4. Bring a large pot of lightly salted water to a boil, add raviolis, and cook about 6 minutes. Drain well.

5. Meanwhile, add to each of 8 fireproof plates 1 ounce gruyere cheese and 1/8 cup heavy cream. Heat under the broiler until the cheese melts then add the raviolis and sprinkle 1 ounce more gruyere on top. Place under the broiler until the cheese browns lightly.

6. Serve the stuffed raviolis on the warm plates.

Spaetzle Ii

Prep Time : 10 Minutes

Cook Time : 15 Minutes

Ready In : 25 Minutes

Servings : 4

"This easy recipe turns eggs and flour into a simple dumpling."

INGREDIENTS:

1 cup all-purpose flour

2 eggs

DIRECTIONS:

Place flour in a medium bowl, making a well for the eggs. Introduce the eggs, and mix with a fork; then knead to form a stiff dough. Pinch off half-inch pieces of batter with fingers, and cook in a large pot of boiling water until dumplings float to the top, 5 to 15 minutes.

Genuine Egg Noodles

Prep Time : 40 Minutes

Cook Time : 10 Minutes

Ready In : 3 Hours 50 Minutes

Servings : 5

"For a delicious change, try making your own fresh and delicious noodles."

INGREDIENTS:

2 cups Durum wheat flour

1/2 teaspoon salt

1/4 teaspoon baking powder

3 eggs

water as needed

DIRECTIONS:

1. Combine flour, salt and baking powder. Mix in eggs and enough water to make the dough workable. Knead dough until stiff. Roll into ball and cut into quarters. Using 1/4 of the dough at a time, roll flat to about 1/8

inch use flour as needed, top and bottom, to prevent sticking. Peel up and roll from one end to the other. Cut roll into 3/8 inch strips. Noodles should be about 4 to 5 inches long depending on how thin it was originally flattened. Let dry for 1 to 3 hours.

2. Cook like any pasta or, instead of drying first cook it fresh but make sure water is boiling and do not allow to stick. It takes practice to do this right.

Plain Pasta

Prep Time : 25 Minutes

Cook Time : 10 Minutes

Ready In : 3 Hours 35 Minutes

Servings : 4

"Real old fashioned homemade pasta. The salt, baking powder and butter are optional. Also, try substituting 1/2 cup milk or 3 beaten eggs for the warm water."

INGREDIENTS:

2 cups semolina flour

1/2 teaspoon salt

1/4 teaspoon baking powder

1/2 cup warm water

1 tablespoon butter

DIRECTIONS:

Mix together flour, salt baking powder. Add warm water and butter; knead dough until stiff. Let rest a few minutes. Roll into a ball and quarter. Using 1/4 of the ball at a time roll out to 1/8 or 1/16 inch thick. Cut into desired shapes. Let dry for 1 to 3 hours on flat surface. Cook as you would pasta

Pasta For Don And His Loves

Prep Time : 30 Minutes

Cook Time : 5 Minutes

Ready In   : 1 Hour 5 Minutes

Servings   : 4

"The soy flour in this version helps to make a tender pasta without eggs or dairy."

INGREDIENTS:

1/3 cup soy flour

1 cup whole wheat flour

1/2 cup spelt flour

3/4 teaspoon salt

1/2 cup water, or as needed

DIRECTIONS:

1. In a medium bowl, stir together the soy flour, whole wheat flour, spelt flour, and salt. Add water, and mix by hand or in a stand mixer with the dough hook attachment. Use more water as needed to form a stiff

but pliable dough. Mix or knead by hand for about 10 minutes. Cover, and let the dough rest for 30 minutes, or if you do not have a pasta machine, rest for at least an hour.

2. Divide dough into four pieces for easier rolling. Run dough through a pasta machine if you have one, or use a rolling pin to roll out very thin, but not transparent on a floured surface.

3. If you are making noodles, allow the pasta sheet to dry for a few minutes. Dust with flour, and roll into a loose tube. Slice the tube into 1/4 inch slices for linguine, or to desired size.

4. To cook: Bring a large pot of lightly salted water to a boil. Add pasta, and cook until al dente, 1 to 5 minutes depending on thickness. Cooked pasta will float to the top of the water.

Spelt Noodles

Servings : 2

"Use your food processor to make fresh pasta for two with white spelt flour, egg and vegetable oil. Roll out the dough through a manual pasta machine, and dry for a few minutes before cutting into shapes."

INGREDIENTS:

1 cup white spelt flour

1 egg

1 tablespoon vegetable oil

3 tablespoons water as needed

DIRECTIONS:

1. (Preferred) Process all ingredients in a food processor until they form a ball that rides on the blades.

2. You can also let a bread machine knead the ingredients for about 5 minutes. (I've never tried this, but have heard it works well.)

3. Pasta can be rolled and cut in a regular (manual, hand-crank) pasta maker by passing it through repeatedly smaller (i.e., higher number) settings until nearly paper thin, and then run through the cutting blades. I am told it does not do so well in an automatic pasta maker.

Vareniky

Prep Time : 30 Minutes

Cook Time : 40 Minutes

Ready In : 1 Hour 55 Minutes

Servings : 6

"These potato- and porcini mushroom-stuffed Ukrainian dumplings are like large ravioli. Serve them with butter and fresh herbs, fried onions, pork cracklings, or sour cream with dill."

INGREDIENTS:

For the Dough:

1 1/2 cups milk

2 tablespoons sunflower seed oil

1 egg yolk

3 1/2 cups all-purpose flour

1/2 teaspoon salt

For the Filling:

3 1/2 ounces dried porcini mushrooms

1/2 cup hot water

1 pound potatoes, peeled

2 onions, chopped

3 tablespoons vegetable oil

salt and pepper to taste

To Cook Vareniky:

1 gallon water

1 tablespoon salt

DIRECTIONS:

1. To mix the dough, combine the milk, sunflower oil, egg yolk, flour, and 1/2 teaspoon salt in a bowl. You can use an electric mixer or knead the dough by hand until it forms a smooth, stiff dough. Shape the dough into a log, wrap it in plastic wrap, and set aside.

2. Soak the dried porcini in 1/2 cup hot water for 45 minutes. Meanwhile, cook the potatoes in boiling salted water to cover until tender, about 20 minutes. Drain and allow to steam dry for a minute or two.

3. Chop the rehydrated mushrooms, reserving the soaking liquid. Mash the potatoes, adding the mushroom-soaking liquid to moisten.

4. Heat the vegetable oil in a skillet over medium heat. Stir in the chopped onions; cook and stir until the onion

has softened and turned translucent, about 5 minutes. Stir in the chopped mushrooms.

5. Mix the mashed potatoes, onions, and mushrooms; season with salt and pepper to taste. Set the filling aside while you roll out the vareniky dough.

6. Cut the dough into discs about 3/8 inch thick and 2 inches wide (1 cm thick and 5 cm in diameter). Flatten or roll each disc on a lightly floured surface to make a thin circle. Drop the filling by tablespoonfuls into the center of each vareniky; fold the dough in half and pinch the edge to seal. Repeat until all of the dumplings are filled.

7. Bring the gallon of water and tablespoon of salt to a boil in a large pot. Add the vareniky to the boiling water and stir once, gently. Simmer until all of the dumplings have floated to the surface, about 10 to 15 minutes. Drain well before serving.

Papa Oriold's Spaetzle

Prep Time : 10 Minutes

Cook Time : 5 Minutes

Ready In   : 15 Minutes

Servings   : 8

"With only 5 ingredients and about 15 minutes, you can make these authentic little German noodles as a great addition to soup or your favorite sauce."

INGREDIENTS:

3 cups all-purpose flour

1 cup cold water

5 eggs, beaten

1 teaspoon salt

1/4 teaspoon baking powder

DIRECTIONS:

1. Mix flour, water, eggs, salt, and baking powder in a bowl until blended.

2. Bring a large pot of water to a boil. Place part of the dough into a spaetzle press or potato ricer. Press dough into boiling water; cook and stir until pasta floats, about 2 minutes. Remove with a slotted spoon and rinse with water; repeat with remaining dough.

Chestnut Pasta

Prep Time   : 50 Minutes

Cook Time : 5 Minutes

Ready In   : 1 Hour 15 Minutes

Servings   : 8

"Chestnuts are no longer just roasted by an open fire. Now, I have a great chestnut pasta recipe. It takes a while to prepare, but it's a labor of love and an unmatched sensation to your taste buds. Enjoy! Buon Appetito!"

INGREDIENTS:

1/2 cup all-purpose flour

1 cup whole wheat flour

1/2 teaspoon salt

1 dash ground nutmeg

1 dash ground black pepper

2 eggs, beaten

2 tablespoons olive oil

1 cup chestnut puree

1/2 cup warm water

1/2 cup olive oil

5 cloves garlic, minced

1/2 cup grated Romano cheese

salt and pepper to taste

DIRECTIONS:

1. In a large bowl, combine flour, whole wheat flour, salt, nutmeg and pepper; mix. Make a well in the center and add eggs and 2 tablespoons olive oil; beat well. In a bowl combine chestnut puree and 1/2 cup water; add to egg mixture. Incorporate flour and egg mix. Dough will be very stiff. Adjust with more flour or water. Knead for 10 minutes and allow dough to rest for 5 minutes.

2. Cut off a handful of dough. With a rolling pin, roll 6 inch wide strips, 1/16" thick. Use a pasta machine if you have one. Dust strips with flour. Allow to slightly dry on muslin cloth. Cut into long pasta 1/4" wide. Dry for 30 minutes.

3. Add pasta to a large pot of rapidly boiling salted water with a tablespoon of oil. Boil for 5 minutes;

drain. Mix pasta with olive oil, minced garlic, Romano cheese, salt and pepper. Serve immediately.

Grandma Randolph's Noodles

Prep Time   : 30 Minutes

Cook Time : 10 Minutes

Ready In   : 2 Hours 40 Minutes

Servings   : 6

"Serve these rustic noodles in place of mashed potatoes with a Thanksgiving dinner, or put them in a turkey carcass soup the day after the feast. Allow a minimum of two hours after cutting for these noodles to dry."

INGREDIENTS:

4 eggs

1 teaspoon salt

1 teaspoon ground black pepper

2 cups all-purpose flour

4 cups beef broth

DIRECTIONS:

1. Beat the eggs and mix in the salt, pepper and flour. Divide the dough into two halves. Roll out the halves to 1/4 inch thick. Let dry for at least 2 hours. Cut the noodles into 1/2 inch to 1 inch wide and as long as you want strips.

2. Drop the noodles into the boiling stock of your choice and boil until soft.

Herb Spaetzle

Prep Time : 10 Minutes

Cook Time : 10 Minutes

Ready In : 20 Minutes

Servings : 6

"Using a spaetzle press or potato ricer makes these seasoned German noodles a breeze to put together."

INGREDIENTS:

4 cups all-purpose flour

2 tablespoons dried basil

1 tablespoon onion powder

salt and ground black pepper to taste

5 eggs

1 3/4 cups water

4 cups water

2 tablespoons salt

DIRECTIONS:

1. Mix flour, basil, and onion powder in a large bowl. Season with salt and black pepper to taste. Make a well in the center of the flour mixture. Whisk eggs and 1 3/4 cups water in another bowl; pour egg mixture into the well and stir until combined. Dough will be thick.

2. Bring 4 cups water and 2 tablespoons salt to a boil in a wide pot. Place part of the dough into a spaetzle press or potato ricer. Press dough into boiling water; cook and stir until pasta is tender, about 1 minutes. Remove pasta with a slotted spoon to a large bowl. Repeat with remaining dough.

Mom's Pasta Dough

Prep Time : 15 Minutes

Ready In : 15 Minutes

Servings : 6

"You'll never buy store-bought pasta again once you learn how quick and easy it is to make homemade pasta dough with just 5 ingredients."

INGREDIENTS:

2 cups all-purpose flour, divided

2 eggs

1 teaspoon olive oil

3/4 teaspoon salt

2 tablespoons warm water, or as needed

DIRECTIONS:

1. Pour 1 3/4 cups flour into a large, shallow bowl and make a well in the center. Crack eggs into the well and mix flour and eggs together with a fork or your hands.

Stir oil and salt into mixture; gradually add water and remaining flour until a dough starts to come together.

2. Knead dough until dough is elastic and soft. Transfer dough to a lightly oiled bowl and cover the bowl with plastic wrap. Store in the refrigerator.

Old School Pasta Dough

Prep Time   : 15 Minutes

Ready In   : 35 Minutes

Servings   : 8

"Homemade pasta dough is easy to make using 5 simple ingredients and is ready in about 30 minutes."

INGREDIENTS:

4 3/4 cups all-purpose flour, or more if needed

4 eggs

6 egg yolks

2 tablespoons extra-virgin olive oil

1/4 teaspoon sea salt

DIRECTIONS:

Mix flour, eggs, egg yolks, olive oil, and salt together in a bowl until dough reaches a crumbly texture. Knead dough until smooth and even. Add 1 tablespoon flour to dough until dough is smooth and soft, if needed.

Wrap dough with a clean cloth or plastic wrap, place in a bowl, and let rest for 20 to 30 minutes. Roll dough into golfball-size balls and roll to about 1/4-inch thickness using a pasta machine or roller.

Easy Homemade Pasta Dough

Prep Time : 20 Minutes

Ready In : 25 Minutes

Servings : 4

"Make your own linguine, ravioli, or any pasta with this recipe to make a consistently delicious and quick homemade pasta dough from scratch."

INGREDIENTS:

2 cups flour

3 large eggs, room temperature

2 tablespoons olive oil

1 teaspoon salt

2 tablespoons water, or as needed

DIRECTIONS:

1. Beat flour, eggs, olive oil, and salt together in a bowl. Add water, 1 teaspoon at a time, to flour mixture until a smooth and very thick dough forms.

2. Turn dough out onto a work surface and knead for 10 minutes. Let dough rest for 5 to 10 minutes. Divide dough into 8 balls and use a pasta machine to roll and cut dough into desired pasta shape.

Tomato Sauce With Sausage

"A meaty sauce with plenty of fresh basil and garlic. A very good sauce that also freezes well."

Serving: 32 | Prep: 25 m | Cook: 45 m | Ready in: 1 h 10 m

Ingredients

- 1/4 cup olive oil
- 2 pounds Italian sausage, casings removed
- 2 large onions, chopped
- 1/4 cup chopped garlic
- 1 (6 ounce) can tomato paste
- 2 (28 ounce) cans whole peeled tomatoes
- 1 cup water
- 1 cup chopped fresh basil
- salt and pepper to taste

Direction

- In a large saucepan heat oil and sauté sausage until brown, about 6 minutes. Add onion and garlic to pot and sauté about 8 minutes. Mix in tomato paste, tomatoes, water and basil. Bring to a boil. Break up tomatoes. Reduce heat to medium and simmer until thickened, about 45 minutes. Season with salt and pepper.

Nutrition Information

- Calories: 101 calories
- Total Fat: 7.2 g
- Cholesterol: 11 mg

- Sodium: 349 mg
- Total Carbohydrate: 5.1 g
- Protein: 4.6 g

Tomatocream Vodka Sauce For Pasta

"Creamy red sauce seasoned Italian-style with garlic, basil, and oregano."

Serving: 8 | Prep: 10 m | Cook: 25 m | Ready in: 35 m

Ingredients

- 4 teaspoons olive oil
- 3/4 clove garlic, minced
- 2 tablespoons vodka
- 1 (14.5 ounce) can Italian-style diced tomatoes, undrained
- 1 1/2 teaspoons dried basil
- 1/4 teaspoon white sugar
- 1/4 teaspoon dried oregano
- 1/4 teaspoon salt
- 1/8 teaspoon ground black pepper
- 1/3 cup milk
- 1/4 cup butter, melted

Direction

- Heat olive oil in a saucepan over medium heat. Cook and stir garlic in hot oil until fragrant, about 1 minute; add vodka, bring to a simmer, and cook until mostly evaporated, about 10 minutes.
- Stir tomatoes, basil, sugar, oregano, salt, and pepper with the garlic and vodka in the saucepan;

bring to a boil and cook until most of the liquid evaporates, about 5 minutes. Remove saucepan from heat.
- Stir milk and butter together in a bowl until smooth; pour into tomato sauce and stir until the color is even.
- Place saucepan over medium-low heat, bring sauce to a simmer, and cook until slightly thickened, about 5 minutes.

Nutrition Information
- Calories: 97 calories
- Total Fat: 8.3 g
- Cholesterol: 16 mg
- Sodium: 198 mg
- Total Carbohydrate: 2.5 g
- Protein: 0.9 g

Tommys Tomato Gravy

"Delicious Southern-style gravy to serve over biscuits or rice. It's been my youngest son's favorite since he was a little boy. Serve while still hot!"

Serving: 10 | Prep: 10 m | Cook: 15 m | Ready in: 25 m

Ingredients
- 2 teaspoons white sugar
- 1 (16 ounce) can crushed tomatoes
- 3 1/2 tablespoons self-rising flour
- 1/2 teaspoon salt

- 1/2 teaspoon ground black pepper
- 2 1/2 tablespoons margarine
- 1 1/2 cups milk

Direction

- Sprinkle sugar directly into opened can of tomatoes. Mix flour, salt, and black pepper together in a small bowl.
- Heat margarine in a large skillet over medium-low heat. Sprinkle flour mixture into melted margarine, stirring constantly. Increase heat to medium-high; continue stirring flour mixture until dissolved and bubbling, 5 to 10 minutes. Add tomatoes; cook and stir until flour mixture is fully incorporated, about 5 minutes.
- Stir milk, 2 to 3 tablespoons at a time, into tomato mixture; increase heat to high. Cook and stir sauce until warm and thickened, 2 to 3 minutes.

Nutrition Information

- Calories: 63 calories
- Total Fat: 3.5 g
- Cholesterol: 3 mg
- Sodium: 261 mg
- Total Carbohydrate: 6.5 g
- Protein: 1.9 g

Turkey Bolognese Recipe

"This is a lighter Bolognese with all the flavor made with lean ground turkey. Mix with freshly boiled pasta."

Serving: 4 | Prep: 20 m | Cook: 50 m | Ready in: 1 h 10 m

Ingredients

- 1 tablespoon olive oil
- 1 onion, diced
- 2 carrots, diced, or more to taste
- 2 stalks celery, diced
- 8 cloves garlic, diced
- 1 pound lean ground turkey
- 1 pinch salt to taste
- 1 pinch garlic powder, or to taste
- 1 pinch onion powder, or to taste
- 1 pinch dried oregano, or to taste
- 1 pinch red pepper flakes, or to taste
- 1 1/2 cups white wine
- 1 (28 ounce) can diced tomatoes
- 2 cups hot water, or more to taste
- 2 tablespoons ketchup, or more to taste

Direction

- Heat olive oil in a large pot over medium heat. Add onion, carrots, and celery; cook and stir until starting to brown, about 10 minutes. Stir in garlic; cook until fragrant, 1 to 2 minutes. Add turkey; season with salt, garlic powder, onion powder, oregano, and red pepper flakes. Cook and stir until turkey is starting to brown, 5 to 8 minutes.
- Pour white wine into the pot and scrape any browned bits off the bottom with a wooden spoon.

Stir in tomatoes, hot water, and ketchup. Simmer until flavors combine, about 30 minutes.

Nutrition Information

- Calories: 374 calories
- Total Fat: 12.2 g
- Cholesterol: 84 mg
- Sodium: 547 mg
- Total Carbohydrate: 22.8 g
- Protein: 25.9 g

Turkey Pasta Sauce

"A tangy, deep tomato meat sauce for pasta, made with ground turkey."

Serving: 14 | Prep: 10 m | Cook: 1 h 12 m | Ready in: 1 h 22 m

Ingredients

- 2 tablespoons extra-virgin olive oil
- 1 large onion, diced
- salt and ground black pepper to taste
- 1 1/4 pounds ground turkey
- 1 tablespoon chopped garlic
- 1 1/2 teaspoons red pepper flakes
- 2 (28 ounce) cans crushed tomatoes
- 1 cup dry white wine
- 1 (6 ounce) can tomato paste
- 1 tablespoon dried oregano
- 1 tablespoon dried basil
- 2 tablespoons white sugar, or more to taste

Direction
- Heat olive oil in a large pot over medium heat. Add onion and a pinch of salt; cook and stir until softened, about 5 minutes. Add turkey; cook and stir until browned, about 5 minutes. Stir in garlic; cook for 2 minutes. Add red pepper flakes.
- Stir tomatoes, white wine, tomato paste, oregano, and basil into the pot. Simmer, stirring occasionally, until the raw wine flavor cooks off, about 1 hour. Stir in sugar to reduce acidity. Season with salt and pepper. Puree sauce with an immersion blender for a less chunky sauce.

Nutrition Information
- Calories: 152 calories
- Total Fat: 5.5 g
- Cholesterol: 30 mg
- Sodium: 279 mg
- Total Carbohydrate: 14.5 g
- Protein: 10.7 g

Tuscan Sausage Ragu

"A thick, rich meat sauce excellent with rigatoni, rotelle or any other thick pasta."

Serving: 10 | Prep: 20 m | Cook: 6 h 15 m | Ready in: 6 h 35 m

Ingredients
- 2 tablespoons olive oil
- 1 pound bulk sweet Italian sausage

- 1 pound bulk hot Italian sausage
- 1 large red onion, diced
- 2 ribs celery, diced
- 3 cloves garlic, minced
- 1/2 cup dry red wine
- 1 (28 ounce) can Italian-style diced tomatoes, undrained
- 1 (28 ounce) can tomato sauce
- salt to taste
- 1 cup heavy cream

Direction

- Heat the olive oil in a large skillet over medium heat. Cook and stir the sweet and hot Italian sausage until browned, about 10 minutes. Break the meat up into crumbles as it cooks. Stir in the onion, celery, and garlic; cook and stir until the onion is translucent, about 8 more minutes. Pour the mixture into a slow cooker. Pour red wine into the skillet, and stir to dissolve the brown flavor bits from the bottom of the skillet. Pour the wine into the slow cooker. Add the diced tomatoes, tomato sauce, and salt to taste. Mix well.
- Cover the slow cooker, set to Low, and cook for 5 hours. Pour in the cream, stir, cover, and cook for 1 more hour. Adjust salt again if necessary, and serve.

Nutrition Information

- Calories: 370 calories
- Total Fat: 28.3 g
- Cholesterol: 75 mg
- Sodium: 1226 mg

- Total Carbohydrate: 11.8 g
- Protein: 14.8 g

Versatile Tomato Sauce

"This delicious tomato and meat sauce can be used for spaghetti or lasagna. The pepperoni gives this sauce an extra kick."

Serving: 6 | Prep: 10 m | Cook: 45 m | Ready in: 55 m

Ingredients

- 3 tablespoons olive oil
- 1 onion, chopped
- 4 cloves garlic, minced
- 1 pound lean ground beef
- 2 (29 ounce) cans tomato sauce
- 1 (14.5 ounce) can stewed tomatoes
- 1/2 pound pepperoni sausage, sliced
- 1 green bell pepper, chopped
- 1 (4.5 ounce) can mushrooms, drained and chopped
- 1/4 teaspoon garlic salt
- 1/4 teaspoon salt
- 1/4 teaspoon ground black pepper
- 1/4 teaspoon onion powder
- 1/4 teaspoon dried oregano
- 1/4 teaspoon Italian seasoning

Direction

- In a medium skillet over medium heat, warm oil and sauté onions and garlic until caramelized; set aside.
- In a large skillet over medium heat, cook ground beef until almost browned. Add onions and garlic and cook for 3 minutes.
- In a large pot over medium heat, combine tomato sauce and stewed tomatoes; bring to a boil and then reduce heat. Simmer sauce for 15 minutes.
- Stir pepperoni, ground beef mixture and green peppers into sauce; cover and simmer for 30 minutes.
- Stir in mushrooms, garlic salt, salt, ground black pepper, onion powder, oregano and Italian seasoning. Simmer for 10 minutes and serve.

Nutrition Information
- Calories: 549 calories
- Total Fat: 39.8 g
- Cholesterol: 96 mg
- Sodium: 2509 mg
- Total Carbohydrate: 23.3 g
- Protein: 27.1 g

www.ingramcontent.com/pod-product-compliance
Lightning Source LLC
Chambersburg PA
CBHW071437070526
44578CB00001B/121